THE WORLDE
AND THE CHYLDE

THE WORLDE
AND THE CHYLDE

Edited by Clifford Davidson and Peter Happé

*With an Appendix on the Dialect
by Paul A. Johnston, Jr.*

EARLY DRAMA, ART, AND MUSIC
MONOGRAPH SERIES, 26

Medieval Institute Publications

WESTERN MICHIGAN UNIVERSITY

Kalamazoo, Michigan
1999

ISBN 1-58044-051-7 (casebound)
ISBN 1-58044-052-5 (paperbound)

Cataloging-in-Publication Data

World and the child.
  The worlde and the chylde / edited by Clifford Davidson and Peter
Happé ; with an appendix on the dialect by Paul A. Johnston, Jr.
    p. cm. -- (Early drama, art, and music monograph series ; 26)
  Includes bibliographical references (p.).
  ISBN 1-58044-051-7 (casebound : alk. paper). -- ISBN 1-58044-052-5
(pbk. : alk. paper)
    1. Moralities, English. 2. English language--Early modern,
1500-1700--Dialects. I. Davidson, Clifford. II. Happé, Peter.
III. Title. IV. Series.
PR2411.W8 1999
822'.2--dc21   99-43610
                                                       CIP

Contents

Illustrations

vii

Acknowledgments

Initially, the editors wish to acknowledge those who have revived *The Worlde and the Chylde* on stage in recent years, especially the Poculi Ludique Societas and its production at the Colloquium sponsored by the Société Internationale pour l'Etude du Théâtré Médiévale at Dublin in 1980 which both of us saw. The play has interest as one of the earliest plays to be published in England, but it also is a very worthy theatrical piece in its own right. Further, its handling of Ages of Man iconography makes it an important document in other ways as well. We are grateful to the Library of Trinity College, Dublin, for allowing us to reprint the text from the unique copy in its possession and to use as illustrations the title page and the printer's mark of its printer, Wynkyn de Worde.

We are grateful also to the staffs of the University of Michigan Library; the Warburg Institute Library; the British Library; the Library of Michigan State University; the Western Michigan University Library; the Cambridge University Library; the Bodleian Library, Oxford; and the Library of the University of Southampton as well as the National Monuments Record. Marianne Cappelletti provided graphics, and Jayne Cappelletti was responsible for the map of London. Paul A. Johnston, Jr., not only advised us on matters of dialect but also produced the account that appears in Appendix III. David Klausner of the Poculi Ludique Societas, David Bevington, Alan H. Nelson, and others gave invaluable information about modern productions and other matters.

Clifford Davidson
Peter Happé

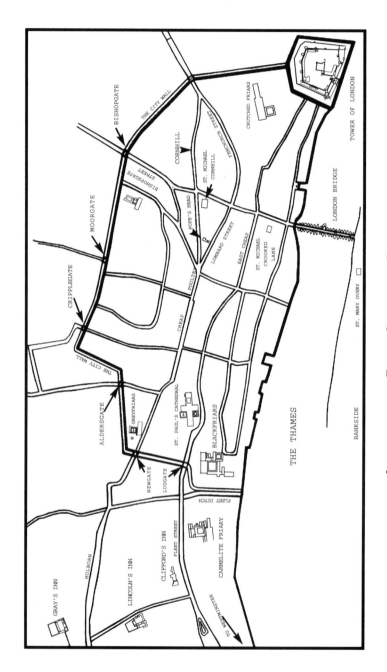

LONDON IN THE EARLY SIXTEENTH CENTURY

Introduction

The study of a play such as *The Worlde and the Chylde,
Otherwyse Called Mundus et Infans* provides an opportunity for
inquiring into a late-medieval theatrical genre as well as the visual
culture of the time. Such an approach will provide evidence of
continuities and reciprocity between art forms, which in turn both
reflected and contributed to the life of late medieval England. The
play is one that today is normally called a "morality," though this
term is based on a very small number of examples and its value has
perhaps been inhibited by a tendency to see them as homogeneous,
using the same methods and structures.[1] In fact these plays were
very different in style and scope, and one of the purposes of the
present edition of *The Worlde and the Chylde* is to show similarities
within this handful of early plays written over a period of over a
hundred years as well as to emphasize its individual distinctiveness.
The present project will also involve attention to the iconographical
culture which, along with the current theatrical traditions, informs
the play under consideration. Pamela Sheingorn has implied that
structurally the late medieval theater may be considered to be one
of the visual arts,[2] and this dimension facilitated its use of the
seeing eye to bring out much that was felt in terms of language and
dramatic performance. We shall note in the discussion of sources
how this play has an unusually close association with the poem entitled *The Mirror of the Periods of Man's Life*, but the visual effects
of the performance of the play itself must in a physical way have
embodied many reminders of what could also be seen in such other
media as wall paintings, woodcuts, and manuscript illuminations. In
every discernible aspect *The Worlde and the Chylde* is a pre-
Reformation play which needs to be seen as consonant with the
visual orientation of traditional religion of late medieval England
that has been described by Eamon Duffy.[3]

TEXT, DATE, AND AUSPICES. The unique copy of *A Propre New
Interlude of the Worlde and the Chylde, Otherwyse Called Mundus
et Infans*, in the Library of Trinity College, Dublin (shelf mark Press

1

A.4.8), was printed as a quarto in black letter by Wynkyn de Worde at the sign of the Sun in Fleet Street (see figs. 1–2), and collates:

$$4° \ A^6B^4C^8 \ (18 \text{ leaves unnumbered})$$

The text is efficiently printed with only a handful of palpable errors (see Textual Notes). Apart from the quire signatures it was not numbered originally, but two penciled number sequences by sheet (1–18) and by page (1–36) have been added. There are no catch words, and the text is devoid of punctuation except for a few virgules in lists. There has been some cropping of the original, but this has not resulted in the loss of anything of significance. Traces of gilt appear on the outer edges of the pages. A note fixed into the Dublin copy records that the book was restored and rebound in January 1982. The rebinding has made a number of readings more certain than appeared in the facsimile which was issued under the editorship of James S. Farmer in the Tudor Facsimile Texts series in 1909. The colophon bears the date 17 July 1522, and as such the drama has special interest as one of the earliest surviving playtexts in English. W. W. Greg places it as no. 5 in his chronological list in *A Bibliography of English Printed Drama*, but since he counts Henry Medwall's *Fulgens and Lucres* as nos. 1 and 2, *The Worlde and the Chylde* is actually fourth in order.[4]

In this early period de Worde is known to have printed some other plays—*Hickscorner* (c.1515–16), *Temperance* (c.1528), and *The Interlude of Youth* (c.1530).[5] As Greg's conjectured date for *Fulgens and Lucres* is as late as 1512–16, it is quite possible that de Worde's printing of *Hickscorner* precedes it. In other words, our text of *The Worlde and the Chylde* is unquestionably one of the very earliest printed plays, and its printer may have been the first to have undertaken any such enterprise in England. Possibly also there may have been a printing of *The Worlde and the Chylde* earlier than 1522 since the Oxford bookseller John Dorne offered "mundus a play" for sale on 7 November 1520,[6] but this was not necessarily the same work or even a product of de Worde's press.

In view of these features of dating and chronology, *The Worlde and the Chylde* has, in comparison with much that was to come in later years, very few indications that it was printed for actors or for persons we should nowadays call directors. If de Worde was indeed one of the innovators in printing plays, it does not follow that he undertook this task in order to attract actors or to encourage play production, especially since we cannot point to a well-established theatrical enterprise hungry for texts of the kind established by Philip Henslowe at the Rose near the end of the sixteenth century. The printing was more likely meant as a contribution to the body of moralizing, devotional, and meditational reading matter that was accumulating, like books of hours and primers, *The Craft to Liue Well and to Die Well* issued by de Worde's press in 1505, or portions of *The Kalender of Shepherds*, which went through several editions, including one by de Worde in 1528.[7] As we shall show, there are dramatic features deeply embedded in the text which notably include a skilled plan for doubling and a number of costume changes that would have been remarkably effective on stage. But it is perfectly possible to regard these as theatrical fossils, so to speak, incorporated at a primary stage in the writing of the text, which itself became, in the act of being printed, directed to other purposes. The absence of stage directions is significant and supportive of such a view. At this early stage of printing plays, de Worde, like the other early printers John Rastell, Richard Pynson, and John Skot, had to create a readership and evolve conventions of presentation. Whether it was worthwhile aiming at an audience of theater people—if there were any who might at that time want to purchase printed playtexts —remains problematic. Later in the sixteenth century when phrases such as "Fouré men may well and easelye playe thys Interlude" (*Impatient Poverty*, 1560) or "As it was sundry times acted by the *Right honorable the Earle of* Pembrook his seruaunts" (*The Taming of a Shrew*, 1594) appeared on title pages, the market had changed, and the presentation of playtexts was correspondingly modified in such a way that printers could appeal to actors or to members of previous audiences who might want to read them. *The Worlde and the Chylde* was thus published in a very special context for the printing of plays.

Ian Lancashire has suggested that the issuing of *The Worlde and the Chylde* by de Worde's press in 1522 was in some way associated with the visit of the Emperor Charles V to London in May to July of that year,[8] but in spite of the impressive woodcut of approximately 86 x 70 cm. on the title page which shows an emperor or king seated on a throne under a canopy and holding an orb and scepter (fig. 1),[9] the moral criticism directed against such rulers within the play would have made this a rather backhanded compliment. In any case, the woodcut was not new but had been previously used by de Worde in an edition of the *Gesta Romanorum* published before 1518, at which time the borders were less worn away than in 1522 when it was reused for *The Worlde and the Chylde*.[10] Speculation about the date of the composition has tended to suggest that the play may have been written and performed at least fourteen or fifteen years earlier than the date of publication. In particular, Lancashire has proposed, on the basis of the reference to St. Stephen (l. 260) whose feast falls on 26 December, that the play was performed at Christmastide—a proposition that he strengthened by noting the importance of Folye as a possible reflection of the Feast of Fools.[11] There is, however, little doubt from the text, as we shall see below, that the performance was indoors, and the most likely location was the great hall belonging to a magnate.[12] As to the year, T. W. Craik's proposal of 1508 is unsupported,[13] though Lancashire has developed it by associating the play with an attack upon William Empson and Edmund Dudley, Henry VII's unpopular administrators, who were at their most active between 1502 and Henry's death in 1509.[14]

Nevertheless, a date even earlier than 1508 for composition and performance may be suggested by some of the references to places conquered by Manhode. Five of these places—Samers, Pycardye, Caleys, Artoys, Flaunders—listed at lines 245–49 are consonant with Henry VII's campaign in France in 1489–92.[15] These, together with Edward H. Sugden's identification of references in the same passage to the suppression of rebels in Kent and Cornwall, might increase the likelihood that the origin of the play is in the reign of Henry VII.[16] The Kent and Cornwall campaigns might thus be indicative of the invasions of Perkin Warbeck in 1495 and 1497. But of the thirteen items in the list, five have still to be adequately accounted for: Salerne, India the Less, Pountes, Florence, and Gascoyne. As the organizing principle of the list is alliterative, the items are not collected in a way that gives much support to an argument for a specific date for the play. Such lists are indeed a conventional feature of boasts, which have analogues in other morality plays and in the boast of Satan in the Temptation of Christ in mystery cycles;[17] thus they do not necessarily carry topical reference.

A further attribution by Lancashire suggests that Manhode may be identifiable with Richard Grey, thirteenth earl of Kent (?1484–1523), who suffered at the hands of Dudley. There is a resemblance in that Grey is known to have been a gambler and one who indulged in tournaments in an extravagant manner (see "sportynge of playe," l. 469). The detail that Folye knows how to "bynde a syue" (l. 538) corresponds with the allegation that Empson's father was a sieve-maker.[18] But it must be said that the links are tenuous, and there is still the puzzle that if these issues are raised in the play it is done in a very limited way. The main intention instead seems to point toward moral teaching rather than any sort of comment upon a political situation. The focus on the allegorical structures to be de-scribed below seems far more emphatic and sustained. However, we shall refer below to some comparable devices in the structure of *Youth* and *Hickscorner* which are contemporary.

The writer of *The Worlde and the Chylde* was very interested in London, but in spite of a number of details which reflect this in-terest, the references to the City and its environment are all con-centrated in the second half of the play. It is here that the allegory is concerned to show that the City is an appropriate place for folly and sin, and although there are references to a number of specific locations within it, most of these would appear to be rather con-ventional. Much of the perception of moral truth takes place away from the City, and the downfall of Manhode has to be portrayed as taking place within it, the journey there being symptomatic and disastrous: "to London to seke Folye wyll I fare" (l. 708). Folye's role in the play, as we shall see, has links with the topos of the ubi-quity of Fools, and he informs Manhode that although he and his ancestors have long dwelled in England, his "chefe dwellynge" there is London (ll. 567–69). Age, having been "In London many a daye" (l. 787) since Folye had led him into self-indulgence, eventu-ally comes to lament his folly. Most of the places mentioned are of ill-repute. Folye was born in Holborn (l. 571), and has spent some time in Westminster, which was known, like Holborn, as the haunt of lawyers as well as being a place of sanctuary for unsavory char-acters. The sensual excesses offered by the City are exemplified by dining in Eastcheap, gambling in Lombard Street, drinking in near-by Pope's Head Alley (ll. 671–73) and other "innes" (l. 585), and visiting the stews in Southwark, across London Bridge (ll. 591–92). For not paying his debts Age is set in the stocks and locked up in Newgate Prison (ll. 790–91) (see figs. 3–5 and Map).

The references to the wickedness of London life are hardly evi-dence that the play originated in London; nevertheless, the author was certainly interested in making the most of the conventional vices of the City. The wickedness of London was already well established as a dramatic and poetic convention, as for example in Langland's *Piers Plowman*, and long it remained so, as Ben Jonson's *The Devil Is an Ass* still bore witness in 1616. Other aspects, particularly the language, may point to a provenance outside of London, but, since the action makes an issue of it, the point of origin may well be only a day's journey from the metropolis (l. 669). The linguistic evidence given in Appendix III suggests a provenance within East Anglia. Thus the origin of the play was probably a considerable distance from Richard Grey's seat at Ampthill in Bedfordshire (around forty miles north of London).

SOURCES AND ANALOGUES. As Henry Noble MacCracken pointed out many years ago, *The Worlde and the Chylde* has a special relationship with the fifteenth-century poem *The Mirror of the Periods of Man's Life*.[19] The similarities arise both in general structure and in a considerable number of individual linguistic features. There is no need to repeat here all the details given by MacCracken, but there are striking verbal parallels concentrated at the beginning of life in poem and play. These include the ideas that "In game he is bigoten in synne" and that at the time of birth mother and child "In perelle of deeþ ben boþe two."[20] Later in the poem the Wicked Angel says, "while þou art a child,/ With þi tunge on folk þou bleere" (ll. 77–78), suggesting line 83 in the play. Most noticeable is the poem's phrase "Lust, liking, & iolite" (l. 35), which reappears as one of the names given to the play's protagonist (l. 125).[21]

Structurally the idea that Folye embodies the Deadly Sins appears in both poem and play, and the function of Conscyence is broadly similar, including, as noted by MacCracken, his comment on the repentant sinner: "Of such a man God is moore gladde/ Þan of a child þat neuere dide synne."[22] In both poem and play the Seven Deadly Sins are rehearsed. In the play these do not appear on stage but are described by Mundus as having the status of kings (ll. 170–83). However, since these Sins are to be found so generally in medieval homilies, art, and drama,[23] it is inappropriate to claim that the dramatist necessarily derived them from *The Mirror of the Periods of Man's Life*. Nevertheless, the closeness of the two texts gives a special advantage when one approaches the decisions made by the dramatist in adapting this material for the stage.

To this we must add, however, that the idea of the Deadly Sins as *kings* does indeed appear elsewhere. This iconography may well be related, for example, to the martial role they play under their leaders, the Infernal Trinity of World, Flesh, and Devil,[24] in the assault in *The Castle of Perseverance*. Earlier in the tradition of the castle figure the Sins are named as kings themselves, as in *Le Songe du Castel* (Picardy, c.1300) where the allegory is that the Castle, which is interpreted within the poem to represent the body of a person, is in the possession of a king called Monde (World). He watches without interfering while seven kings, named as the Seven Deadly Sins, carry out an assault and take possession of the body-castle. After some revelry to celebrate their victory, another hideous and completely black king (*Tous noirs*) rides up on a black horse, closes up the castle, and casts it upon the ground; he is identified as Death.[25]

Less close to *The Worlde and the Chylde* than *The Mirror of the Periods of Man's Life* is the poem *Of þe Seuen Ages* from an early fifteenth-century Carthusian manuscript (British Library MS. Add. 37,049, fols. 28ᵛ–29ʳ). It will be seen that both poem and play draw on the same iconography. The poem, identified by Alan H. Nelson as a significant analogue also for *The Castle of Perseverance*, shows a progressively aging mankind figure from birth to death.[26] Illustrations of each of the seven stages of life are inserted into the text and its margins (fig. 6). At the top of fol. 28ᵛ the infant is naked in a cradle, beneath which is a simply clothed and barefoot child between his guardian angel on his right and his attendant demon on his left. The text of the poem begins with the words "Nakyd in to þis warlde borne am I"—words that provide an interesting analogy with Infans' announcement that his mother has sent him "in to the worlde . . ./ Poore and naked as ye may se" (ll. 44–45). In the next stage, boyhood, the poem says that he will "go play with my felowe," while *The Worlde and the Chylde* is more specific about his activities. The poem's youth, smartly attired, with shoes and cap, will "play and rage" with women, with which we may compare the play's protagonist in his seeking of "All loue longynge in lewdnes" (l. 128). Then, in the poem, the man wears rich clothing and carries an axe; he next appears as a merchant with a fashionable hat and a money-bag. The old man wears a black hood and carries a rosary, while in the final illustration an angel snatches away the soul of the dying man as the bad angel, opposite, turns away in frustration. The import of the sequence is given most emphatically by this final illustration in that it represents the outcome as salvation. This highly schematized structure is not, however, followed meticulously by the playwright.

Turning to the dramatic context of the play in its own time, we have noted that among the early morality plays *The Worlde and the Chylde* stands as one of the very earliest of this genre to be printed. The Macro plays (*The Castle of Perseverance*, *Mankind*, and *Wisdom*) all survive only in manuscript, as does Thomas Chaundler's Latin play *Liber Apologeticus*.[27] *The Pride of Life* was also in manuscript, but now only a photograph survives.[28] Henry Medwall's *Nature* was almost certainly written before *The Worlde and the Chylde*, but it was not printed until c.1530 (by William Rastall), and the printing of John Skelton's *Magnyfycence*, perhaps written by 1519, was delayed until roughly the same year.[29] Thus, though it shares with other moralities its preoccupation with salvation and repentance, the dramatist's inheritance could hardly have been from printed play texts but much more substantially from the conventions of performance, from the visual arts, and from the didactic and homiletic traditions of the medieval Church.

With regard to performance, we can be sure from the evidence in the volumes already issued in the Records of Early English Drama project that there were numerous and frequent entertainments in great houses and also a substantial amount of parish drama, performed either in the streets or indoors, even though few texts survive.[30] The provenance of *The Worlde and the Chylde* seems to lie in the former type of presentation, though the technical requirements are very few indeed, and the play could have been done almost anywhere. In spite of some possible references to public affairs, however, it is less clearly to be associated with a performance at Court than *Magnyfycence*. The play's most remarkable attribute is its design as a play almost certainly written for only two players. This construction is skillfully managed, and there is adequate provision of time for the necessary changes of costume between episodes.[31]

In terms of its allegory *The Worlde and the Chylde* has similarities with the plays mentioned above, though the degree of correspondence varies. With *The Castle of Perseverance* it shares the important idea that mankind must necessarily be involved with the

World even though this implies a condition of sinfulness inherited from Adam. As a result of the Fall, life must be a trial. Thus Mundus, on his scaffold in *The Castle of Perseverance*, eagerly welcomes Humanum Genus,[32] and it is through Mundus, one of the three Enemies of Man, that the protagonist of *The Castle of Perseverance* encounters sins. In that play special influence is given to Covetous, who also has a separate scaffold and who twice brings Humanum Genus into jeopardy. Eventually the latter receives mercy because at the last moment of his life he begs for it.

Closer to *The Worlde and the Chylde* in date is Medwall's *Nature*, a play intended for indoor performance and presumably associated with a meal since it is divided into two convenient parts. The motif of submission to the World is again present here. Nature, who is essentially Man's good advisor, introduces him into the World's presence: "Lo yender the World whyche thou must nedys to!" (1.236). Later Reason refers to the World as one of the Three Enemies of Man (2.13), and he characterizes the way temptation works:

> Fyrst doth the World geve us an allectyfe
> To covet ryches and worldly renown,
> Wyth other vanyteys that be used in thys lyfe. (2.16–18)

The World gives Man "thys place," by which he means his own throne (1.471). In saying "I gyve you here auctoryte and power/ Over all thynge"(1.472–73) he picks up on the idea that it is man who exercises sovereignty over all worldly things (1.117–19)—a motif we shall find of importance in considering the allegory and iconography of *The Worlde and the Chylde*—and later at lines 462– 64 he gives Man a "garment," hat, and "gurdell" which may have regal connotations.

The action of the second part of *Nature* gives much scope to the Deadly Sins. Led by Sensuality and Bodily Lust, they succeed in separating Man from Reason. The business and scope of these episodes are more complex and the sins more individualized than the description of the seven kings in *The Worlde and the Chylde*, but the turning point comes with the allegory of Age. While this personification does not actually appear on stage, Sensuality nevertheless gives a description redolent with emblematic detail—a description which in its typology comes very near to the central concerns of *The Worlde and the Chylde*:

> Hys stomak faynteth every day,
> Hys bak croketh, hys hed waxeth gray,
>   Hys nose droppeth among,
> Hys lust ys gone and hys lykyng. (2.943–46)

Thus the failing of physical powers and the loss of (sexual) drive bring on the final crisis, which in *Nature,* as in *The Worlde and the Chylde*, leads through repentance to salvation.[33] Though *Everyman* derives from a Dutch source, the English version, which is known to have been printed at least four times in the first years of the sixteenth century, apparently had a special appeal as a "treatyse" to aid the dying.[34] *Everyman*'s popularity may be a reflection of this very sense of human weakness and vulnerability which nevertheless sees salvation as attainable through the coming of death. The composition of *The Worlde and the Chylde* may be understood as another response to such fundamental human frailty.

Salvation is ultimately achieved in *Nature* and *The Worlde and the Chylde*, as it is in *The Castle of Perseverance*, through a structure in which the protagonist falls twice. Manhode, the hero of *The Worlde and the Chylde*, is first rescued by Conscyence, who separates him from the kings introduced by Mundus—an episode culminating in "For Conscyence clere I clepe my kynge" (l. 502). Thereafter his second fall, induced by Folye, will form the second part of the play. We shall see that this seam or join in the structure has some importance in the interpretation of the play. A markedly similar effect appears in *The Castle of Perseverance* where the repetition of the protagonist's fall is managed by Covetous, who thus appears to be the dominating vice. Quite remarkably in *The Worlde and the Chylde*, even though economy over acting resources was a consideration, the dramatist also developed the benefit of this double fall and rise structure in a way which is fundamental to his dramaturgy.

THE ALLEGORY. The allegorical method shared by the plays considered above has been much misunderstood. The prejudice against allegory was articulated by Coleridge when he wrongly identified it in his *Statesmen's Manual* as "but a translation of abstract notions into a picture-language, which is itself nothing but an abstraction from objects of the senses; the principal being more worthless even than its phantom proxy, both alike insubstantial, and the former shapeless to boot."[35] In no sense does this do justice to

these moralities, which provided dramatizations of perceived experience and were regarded as reflecting a reality beyond and above
the literal sense of the words or the physical gestures of the action.[36]
The function of allegory has come into question recently from
another direction, perhaps under the influence of modern critical
theory which has tended to see a text not as a finite and fixed piece
of meaning so much as a place where different meanings are
brought into relationship with one another. This heuristic ambiguity
is likewise in line with the view expressed by Gay Clifford: the
allegorist, this writer suggests, will assume "that his readers will
understand his narrative, not just as the record of a unique human
experience . . . but as an expression of larger kinds of truth."[37]

The Worlde and the Chylde, along with the other moralities and
many of the later interludes, thus used allegory as a means of
exhibiting permanently conceived religious truths; yet the methodology of all of them usually turns not upon a single allegory but upon
a series of allegorical devices which can be brought into relationship with one another. It is the peculiar relationship of differing
allegorical structures which gives to each text its unique interest.
But even so there still remain, usually, ambiguities in the relationship between allegorical structures. This process is enhanced by the
implicit reference to iconographical material which may help to
bring visually perceived aspects of the religious culture into a
relationship with dramatic realization. While an allegory may be a
figure which stands for some underlying significance, there is so
often the sense that all cannot be comprehensively discovered, and
it is this which gives allegory its peculiar vitality—a vitality which
was as evident in the time of the author of *The Worlde and the
Chylde*, or of *The Faerie Queene*, as it was in the age of the Church
Fathers, for example Origen and Clement of Alexandria. Allegory
revealed, and yet it remained compulsively a mystery or "dark con-
ceit."

In broad terms the allegories of *The Worlde and the Chylde* are
related as follows. The play moves progressively through an allegory of the Ages of Man, but this is subdivided by the double structure which shows the protagonist first overcome by Mundus and
then misled by Folye, who admits that he is linked to Mundus. This
relationship is effective because in a common way Folye is a kind
of manifestation of Mundus: "For Folye is felowe with the Worlde"
(l. 618). However, this broad structure is shot through with a

number of other allegories, of which we may identify one as an allegory of kings, another of names and costumes, and a third as the relationship between Conscyence and Perseveraunce, who perhaps are a counteraction to the Mundus-Folye axis. Finally, there is the constructive allegorical progression from Wanhope through Contrition to the Twelve Articles of Faith which end the play. This list exemplifies an important feature of interlocking allegories which is that the terms do not necessarily contain the same kind of conceptual force, and also that some of them are static and almost emblematic, whereas others have a dynamic function within the action of the play. Moreover inconsistencies in their use are not necessarily faults in construction so much as a feature of how allegories may be exploited differentially.

Let us consider the allegory of kings.[38] The salient feature is the identification by Mundus of the Seven Deadly Sins as kings who follow him (ll. 170–83). They do not actually appear, but the device (for which we have already noted a precedent) is very much a subject of the discourse, to which a return is made from time to time: at a climactic moment, before the appearance of Conscyence, Manhode proclaims their influence when he says, "All those sende me theyr leuery" (l. 281). But Mundus himself is also a king, as his initial self-display is designed to show:

> For I am ruler of realmes I warne you all
> And ouer all fodys I am kynge.
> For I am kynge and well knowen in these realmes rounde.
> I haue also paleys ypyght. (ll. 3–6)
>
> For I am the Worlde, I warn you all,
> Prynce of powere and of plente. (ll. 13–14)

Later Manhode salutes him: "Gramercy, Worlde and emperour" (l. 204). Folye's close relationship with Mundus is neatly pointed when he says that the friars crowned him king (ll. 599–601).

It may well be that the woodcut on the title-page showing a king crowned and robed (fig. 1) was meant to point to this domination by Mundus, but if so there is a contrasting idea in which Manhode himself boasts of his appearance, which is clearly meant to suggest that of a king:

> I am ryall arayde to reuen vnder the ryse.
> I am proudely aparelde in purpure and byse.

> As golde I glyster in gere. (ll. 268–70)

His boasting also recites the names of the countries he has conquered (ll. 245–48). His role as a king, however, is interrelated with
his conception of himself as a "knyght" (l. 249), and chivalry could
naturally be associated with kingship. Connected with this may be
the expressions of fealty which appear more than once.

These evil manifestations of kingship are, however, contrasted
with another strain which attributes virtue to it. Repeatedly Christ
is named as a king, as in Infans's first line: "Cryst our kynge, graunte
you clerly to know þe case" (l. 25). Other references are found at
lines 288, 356, 373, and 862, and, cognate with this, Manhode calls
Conscyence his king (l. 502). Also part of the effect of this elabor-
ate device is that as Conscyence condemns all the wicked seven
kings, one by one, he makes an ironic play on kingship, possibly a
commonplace, when he comes to the last:

> For Couetous I clepe a kynge.
> Syr, Couetous in good doynge
>   Is good in all wyse.
> But, syr knyght, wyll ye do after me
> And Couetous your kynge shall be? (ll. 413–17)

There is nothing unusual in this exploitation of layers of meaning
in an allegorical device: indeed one of the strengths of allegory is
that it lends itself to a constant shifting of focus between one level
and another.

The resemblance of *The Worlde and the Chylde* to the poem
called *Of the Seuen Ages* we have noted is really another manifestation of a variable allegory inasmuch as there appear, in various
literary and iconographical contexts, a range in the number of Ages
from three to twelve.[39] Adolf Katzenellenbogen has pointed out the
importance of the figure seven in a large number of topics, including the requests in the Lord's Prayer, the seven Sacraments, and
the Acts of Mercy, and he takes the interesting step of suggesting a
link of these to the instruction and support of priests.[40] In *The
Worlde and the Chylde* the number seven is not mentioned, though
some of the Ages are seven years long. In fact, the allegory of the
Ages is here interwoven with another common allegorical device:
the giving, explication, and changing of names. The play on names
is supported by the changing of costumes, a procedure deeply em-

bedded in the theatricality of allegory. It has been pointed out by Mallory Chamberlin, Jr., that the speech prefixes Mundus, Infans, and Age never appear in the dialogue and so are not known to the audience, unless the costume and movement help to particularize them.[41]

In the action on stage the Ages are unfolded and identified in the following way. Infans is called a "chylde" (1. 52), and when he goes, at seven years old, to Mundus the latter endorses the name Dalyaunce given by his mother (ll. 55–56) but actually dubs him Wanton for the following period, which lasts until he reaches his fourteenth year (ll. 68–70). For the third Age Mundus gives the name Love, Lust, and Lykynge (1. 125) which apparently ends at "One and twenty," though the age of nineteen has been mentioned previously (ll. 144, 155). At the beginning of the fourth Age Mundus makes him a man, called Manhode (1. 160), and it is here the allegory of the Deadly Sins as kings is introduced. This long phase is more complex, especially as it is not specifically separated or subdivided. Manhode is warned by Conscyence against "Folye and Shame" (1. 489). Sure enough, Folye ostentatiously throws away the attribute Shame in a "cloute" (1. 641). When he has established his dominance he still refers to his victim as "manhode," but now he revives the name Shame for him (ll. 678, 682). Significantly, Manhode sums up his role at this point in a jingling couplet:

> Ye, Folye is my felowe and hath gyuen me a name.
> Conscyence called me Manhode, Folye calleth me Shame. (ll. 700–01)

After Conscyence, observing Manhode's link with Folye, has summoned his brother Perseveraunce, Manhode reappears as an old man. In spite of the speech prefix, he does not give himself this new name, but with pain and shame rehearses those we have mentioned. There is no doubt, however, that he is now pressed by old age (ll. 797–99), as his appearance, posture, and movements presumably show. In his despair he calls for Death. Perseveraunce quickly warns him to beware of Wanhope, and gives him a new name, Repentaunce. After further instruction, notably in the twelve articles of faith which are enumerated, Perseveraunce repeats the name Repentaunce in the last speech of the play (1. 971). Examined from this point of view it appears that there are five Ages, which might be extended to seven if the titles Shame and Repentaunce are counted separately. But it may be argued that the run of the action—

1. Enthroned Emperor or King. Title page of the unique copy of *The Worlde and the Chylde* published by Wynkyn de Worde in 1522. Courtesy of the Board of Trinity College Dublin.

2. Wynkyn de Worde's printer's device, from *The Worlde and the Chylde*. Courtesy of the Board of Trinity College Dublin.

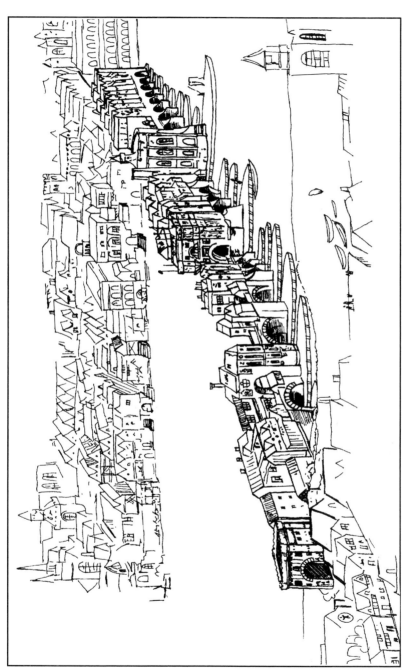

3. London Bridge as it appeared in the early sixteenth century. Drawing by Marianne Cappelletti, based on fifteenth- and sixteenth-century drawings and prints.

4. The Stews, on the south bank of the Thames. Drawing by Marianne Cappelletti, based on an eighteenth-century engraving made from a painting of the Coronation procession of Edward VI in 1547.

5. Newgate Prison. Drawing by Marianne Cappelletti, after an anonymous
eighteenth-century engraving.

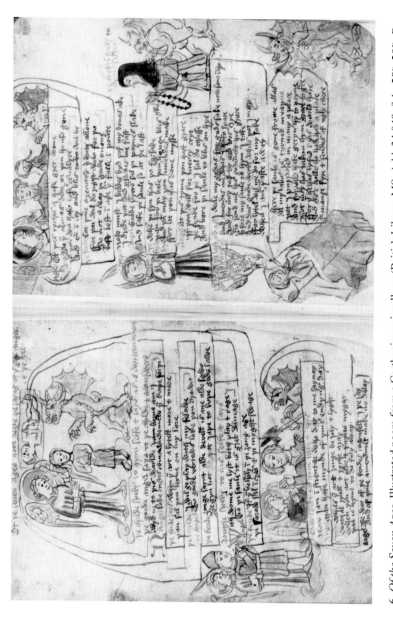

6. *Of the Seuen Ages*. Illustrated poem from a Carthusian miscellany (British Library MS. Add. 34,049, fols. 28ᵛ–29ʳ). By permission of the British Library.

7. The Six Ages of Man. Painted glass roundel (c. 1180), northeast transept, Canterbury Cathedral. RCHME ©Crown Copyright.

8. September, in Twelve Ages of Man series, showing ruined man. Woodcut from *Prymer of Salisbury Use* (Paris: François Regnault, 1529), fol. 14ᵛ. By permission of the Folger Shakespeare Library.

9. The Ages of Man, showing costumes appropriate to each age. Manuscript illumination (14th century), Jacob van Maerlant, *Der Naturen bloeme* (British Library MS. Add. 11,390, fols. 1ᵛ–2ᵗ). By permission of the British Library.

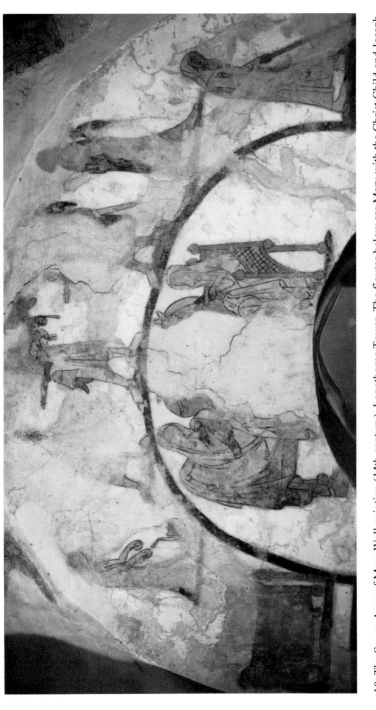

10. The Seven Ages of Man. Wall painting (14th century), Longthorpe Tower. The figures below are Mary with the Christ Child and Joseph. RCHME ©Crown Copyright.

11. The Seven Ages of Man. Manuscript illumination, illustrating Psalm 89 (90). Paris, Bibliothèque Nationale, MS. lat. 8846, fol 161ʳ. By permission of the Bibliothèque Nationale.

12. Children at play, illustrating entry for "Etas" ("Age"). Illumination in James le Palmer, *Omne Bonum* (British Library MS. Royal 6.E.VII, fol. 67ᵛ). By permission of the British Library.

13. The Seven Ages of Man. Manuscript illumination, Bartholomaeus Anglicus, *De Proprietatibus Rerum* (James Ford Bell Library, University of Minnesota), fol. 75ʳ. The center figure at the bottom represents the final stage of life; beneath him is Death. Courtesy of the James Ford Bell Library, University of Minnesota.

14. The Wheel of Life. Manuscript illumination by a Westminster artist (c.1310). Robert de Lisle Psalter (British Library, MS. Arundel 83, fol. 126ᵛ). Instead of Fortune at the center is the head of the Savior, surrounded by the words "Cuncta simul cerno: totum racione guberno" ("I see everything at once, with reason I govern everything"). The Ten Ages of Life are arranged clockwise around the spokes of the wheel from Infancy to Old Age, Death, and Burial Rites, followed at last at the very bottom by the Tomb. By permission of the British Library.

15. King, seated on his throne, and a Fool. Lacock Psalter (mid-13th century). Bodleian Library, MS. Laud Lat. 114, fol. 114ᵛ). Courtesy of the Bodleian Library.

16. Perseverance (Alan Park, at left) and Age (John Mayberry); scene from Poculi Ludique Societas production of *The Worlde and the Chylde* (1979).

17. Gesture of insult, clawing at his "ars" (see
Folye's gesture in *The Worlde and the Chylde*, l.
527), to which is added the exposure of the but-
tocks. Drawing by Marianne Cappelletti, after Jean
Fouquet, Martyrdom of St. Apollonia (detail), in
The Hours of Etienne Chevalier.

the rhythms of the plot, so to speak—seems to counter this, and to settle for five Ages. Though the convention of Seven Ages may have been invoked, this version appears to be a careful and deliberate variation of it.

The last major allegorical structure to be noted here is that of folly. Manhode is warned against Folye early in the play, but his arrival about halfway through changes the theatrical tone and enables the dramatist to introduce new material. The allegory turns upon his presentation of the ubiquity of folly, which had been elaborated in Sebastian Brant's *Narrenschiff* (1495) and its English translation, Alexander Barclay's *Ship of Fools* (1509), a work reissued by de Worde in 1517. *The Worlde and the Chylde*, apparently composed in the first years of the sixteenth century, was written at a time when the idea of folly was being developed and exploited in a number of ways on and off the stage. Erasmus wrote *The Praise of Folly* in 1509 and published it in 1511. Not long thereafter Skelton made impressive use of Fansy and Foly in *Magnyfycence* in which he was probably influenced by the French *Sotties* that were popular at this period.[42] Dramatically the intervention of Skelton's fools is of paramount importance because they change the moral state of Magnyfycence himself, and further Skelton has hit upon the clever device of having two fools with distinctive voices. The extension of the material in *The Worlde and the Chylde* is to the location of London, which appears as the City of wickedness. In this manifestation, Folye himself is evil, and the vigor of his stage presence no doubt helped to set up a continuing allegory of evil which was explored theatrically in the next generation of interludes and beyond, mostly in the character of the Vice.[43]

In *The Worlde and the Chylde* Folye's contribution is to fight a bout of "buckler play" with Manhode, to lead him into the seamy wickedness of London, to comment on this to the audience, to transfer his own name (Shame) to Manhode—and to do all this in lively language and in a lively style which would no doubt have great appeal to the audience. His concentrated use of proverbial expressions (ll. 628–29, 634, 648, 698) and abuse (ll. 624–25) are symptomatic of the change in tone which is brought about. Presumably his costume would also be a feature of his performance.

But beyond these staging functions there is also the possibility that the dramatist saw in Folye, with his ability to sharpen up reference to contemporary matters, a means of hinting at the topical satire proposed by Lancashire. There is no doubt that the allegorical effect of Brant's fools led towards such an interpretation, and the dramatic mode which shows itself in Medwall and Skelton as well as in *Youth* and *Hickscorner* points in the same way. This mode was even further developed by John Heywood in the early 1530s to comment on and presumably to influence the highly dangerous matter of Henry VIII's divorce.

ICONOGRAPHY. The iconographic traditions which were absorbed by the anonymous playwright into *The Worlde and the Chylde* are closely intertwined with the allegory discussed above. In such instances the value of giving close attention to the iconography is that it may reveal how the texts themselves echo and depend upon cultural and theological preoccupations. There is the added benefit that iconography may help to interpret tone and mood, for it gives us pointers about how the text might have been intended or indeed how it might have been received by a readership or an audience already acquainted with and influenced by the implicit and explicit significance of the visual arts. Additionally, the iconography can give useful suggestions about the visual effects that might have been expected in any early performances of the play. The following discussion will concentrate upon two broad topics, the Ages of Man, and Fools, both of which, as we have seen, are essential to the allegorical structures of *The Worlde and the Chylde*.

The Ages of Man, best known today from Jaques' speech in act 2, scene 7 of Shakespeare's *As You Like It*, was a highly popular motif which had been defined early on by St. Augustine and the encyclopedist Isidore of Seville, then later by Thomas Aquinas and others.[44] Isidore's formulation provides the following description, which was to exert strong influence on subsequent iconography:

> The first age is *infantia*, extending from the child's birth into the light of day until the age of seven years. The second age is *pueritia*, that is, pure and not yet old enough to reproduce, and lasts until the fourteenth year. The third is *adolescentia*, an age mature enough for reproduction, lasting until the twenty-eighth year. The fourth, *iuventus*, is the strongest of all the ages, and ends with the fiftieth year. The fifth age is that of riper years, that is to say, of mature judgment, *gravitas*, and is the gradual decline from youth into old age. . . . This age commences with the fiftieth year and ends with the seventieth. *Senectus* is the sixth stage and is bounded by no definite span of years, but whatever of life remains after those earlier five stages is marked up to old age. *Senium* is

the final part of old age, so named because it is the terminus of the sixth age.[45]

The seventh age, then, will involve death or, as in the *Promptorium Parvulorum*, the Resurrection.[46]

Similar stages were given illustration in painted glass in the typological window in the northeast transept of Canterbury Cathedral (fig. 7), where the inscriptions identify six boys and men of increasing age.[47] An important aspect of the iconography in this glass is the way that the circular shape of the roundel is exploited so that figures grow in size, while it also is significant that they are placed opposite and corresponding to a panel showing figures representing the Six Ages of the World.[48] This early window, however, has as its main theme the Wedding at Cana, a connection which is a commonplace[49] but not to our knowledge picked up in later examples of the Ages of Man iconography.

The Ages scheme, in its various variants whether in six or seven stages or otherwise, was widely disseminated in illustrations between the fourteenth century and the 1520s. One set of woodcuts, dividing the ages into twelve corresponding to the months of the year, which conceivably could have been known to the author of *The Worlde and the Chylde* was the popular *Kalender of Shepherds* that was first published in a crude English translation in 1503.[50] Again the figures represent rising and falling fortunes, as also in the twelve-month scheme which appears in a series showing the Ages of Man in illustrations in some printed books of hours of the early sixteenth century.[51] A primer of Salisbury use published in 1529 shows a low point being reached at September (fig. 8) where the man is barefoot and leaning on a stick as he is being chased away from a gate as though he were a vagabond. By the gate is an empty and broken cask, possibly having contained wine, which suggests the mood of decay. In related woodcuts he holds his right hand open as if begging.[52]

One of the attractions of the illustrations of the Ages of Man particularly is the frequent interest in accurate and appropriate circumstantial detail. In an illustration from a fourteenth-century manuscript of Jacob van Maerlant's *Der naturen bloeme* (British Library MS. Add. 11,390, fols. 1^v–2^r), the costumes are given special attention to represent the different stages in life (fig. 9). They follow well established types. The fourth figure, for example, has sword, shield, helmet, and chain-mail, and hence may serve for comparison to the interest in combat and chivalry found in *The Worlde and the Chylde*.

Another fourteenth-century illustration, the wall painting at Longthorpe Tower (fig. 10), shows a carefully balanced sequence consisting of Infans, Puer, Adolescens, Vir, an indecipherable successor, followed by Senectus and Decrepitus.[53] As this is painted in a curve over an arch, the artist has made a special point, not unrelated to representations of rising and falling on Fortune's wheel, by using the physical shape of his painting to show the Vir at the highest point.[54] Like Wanton in *The Worlde and the Chylde*, Puer here plays with a top, and this is a motif which appears in a number of other representations, including the illustration for Psalm 89 (*AV*: 90) in Bibliothèque Nationale MS. 8846, fol. 161ʳ (fig. 11) and a miniature in the *Omne Bonum* (fig. 12).[55] Whipping the top is also the child's activity that is seen in a Four Ages depiction illustrating Bartholomaeus Anglicus, *De proprietatibus rerum* (Bibliothèque Nationale, MS. fr. 22,531, fol. 99ᵛ), which presents the second Age as the central figure, who is a man courting a fashionably dressed woman.[56] The prosperous figure for the third Age looks down reflectively upon what appears to be a money bag, and the last figure, here quite large and dominating, is seated looking downward disconsolately. Illustrating the Ages in another manuscript containing a French translation of Bartholomaeus Anglicus's *De proprietatibus rerum* (James Ford Bell Library MS.) is a Seven Ages illumination (fig. 13). Here the mood is decidedly grim, with Decrepitus centrally placed; beneath him lies a skeletal Death whose barrenness and grimace contrast sharply with the rich clothing of most of the human figures.

There are two implications from the iconography of the Ages which may especially reflect upon *The Worlde and the Chylde*. One involves the manner in which Man, as time unfolds in his lifetime, comes to be represented as a king at his most triumphant moment. In the Robert de Lisle Psalter this pattern is presented in terms of a wheel at the top of which a man figure in a roundel is crowned and sceptered, with his left hand raised to signify power (fig. 14).[57] The Latin phrase which encircles him is "Rex sum rego seculum: mundus est meus totius" ("I am a king, I rule the present world: the whole world is mine"). This text cannot be interpreted to be indicative of a separate allegorical figure—that is, Mundus—but must be designating a man who at this point in his life becomes a king of worldly things within time. But of course the ambivalence that he might become coterminous with Mundus—one of the Three Enemies of Man—is undoubtedly in play.

The second implication arises from the objectives or intentions that inform the Ages of Man in medieval iconography. One strain associates the passing of the Ages with the transitory nature of human experience, and in this instance it is linked with the wheel of Fortune, as in the de Lisle Psalter (fig. 14). The implication is one of *despair* since the turning of the wheel inevitably brings disaster, and such iconography opens up the way to Wanhope, the species of despair from which there is no redemption[58] and which Age approaches closely in *The Worlde and the Chylde*. It is the sin of Judas. But since Age is also capable of bringing wisdom—and one of the purposes of the structure is to open up the possibility of salvation—the last Age may be more spiritual. The claim of Augustine that in senectitude the individual is reborn into spiritual life can be seen represented in the illustration for Psalm 89 (*AV*: 90) in Bibliothèque Nationale, MS. lat. 8846 (fig. 11). In this miniature showing the seven Ages, the penultimate panel depicts the man with two crutches walking miserably with head downward towards a hill; but the hill has flowers and trees upon it. In the seventh scene the elderly man is sitting bare-headed upon a bench, but his whole demeanor has changed: he now looks hopefully upward, both hands raised as if in contemplation of the higher form of life for which he now has expectation. There seems little doubt that the dramatist of *The Worlde and the Chylde* was making use of both these strains. His concept of the Ages was intended as encouragement to adopt spiritual discipline, itself associated with the *ars moriendi*, but at the same time giving hope of salvation through repentance.

The understanding of fools is not unrelated to the iconography which we have discussed above, for the pursuit of self-gratification that is depicted in the passing of a man's years in the Ages of Man scheme is depicted as ultimately foolish and self-defeating in the end when one must face the choice of salvation or damnation. The connection seems present certainly when we examine a woodcut in Sebastian Brant's *Das Narrenschiff* (Basle, 1495) and the copy of this illustration in early editions of Barclay's translation—a woodcut that presents familiar rising and falling figures on Fortune's wheel as having asses' ears and some human hands or feet

along with hooves.[59] The journey of life is not only a passage
through the Ages but also, if one pursues vanity, the possibility of
empty achievement followed by a tumble later. Yet another and
more sinister variation may be the iconography of the Dance of
Death, which shows another side of folly in that Death will provide
the terminus for life in every rank of society from the highest to the
lowest, for Death waits upon all. Below the early sixteenth-century
wall painting of the Dance of Death at Stratford-upon-Avon was a
dead king eaten by worms,[60] a figure warning of the ultimate
foolishness of earthly striving for power. We may also be reminded
of the *transi* tomb, an example of which is Archbishop Chichele's
in Canterbury Cathedral where the churchman is shown at the
height of his authority in his vestments above, and below as an
emaciated corpse, eaten by worms.[61] These related iconographic
motifs all stress the ultimate folly inherent in man's proclivity to
pursue power, wealth, and acts of pride—an idea that would find
particular favor in the early years of the sixteenth century, a time
when Barclay's *Ship of Fools* struck a responsive chord among
readers.

There was, however, an especially strong iconographical tradition which associates fools with kings that developed in psalter
illustrations, especially in connection with Psalm 52 (*AV*: 53), which
begins with the words "Dixit insipiens in corde suo: non est Deus"
("The fool said in his heart, 'There is no God'").[62] So in the Lacock
Psalter (Bodleian Library, MS. Laud Lat. 114) there is an interesting stand-off between two figures, a king (i.e., King David, the
presumed author of the psalms) and a fool (fig. 15). In this case the
latter is wearing a parti-colored costume. Such a garment was not
always worn in pictures, and on stage in the early sixteenth century
the fool, though he may sometimes have worn bright clothing,
would probably have been more often distinguished by a hood and
bells.[63] It is striking, however, that in *The Worlde and the Chylde*
the activities of Folye have a special function in the narrative. He is
used as a symbolic representative of human folly, but he also appears dynamically within the plot of the play as the means by which
Manhode is brought to Shame. The iconographical tradition gives
ample scope to the wickedness located in human folly.

LANGUAGE AND VERSIFICATION. The dialect of *The Worlde and
the Chylde* will be examined in Appendix III, which contains a sur-

vey by Paul A. Johnston, Jr., of the linguistic evidence for the provenance of the play. Johnston tentatively places the play in Cambridgeshire, perhaps even in the city of Cambridge, but also notes various East Anglian characteristics. Determination of the dialect in this case is made more difficult by the introduction of London Chancery English in the print shop, but evidence of the underlying dialect must appear in the nature of the rhymes. These then can be studied with the assistance of the *Linguistic Atlas of Later Medieval English*,[64] which, though it purports to survey dialects only up to 1450, provides some parameters for the geographic distribution of the linguistic forms of the language of the play. While there seems here to be no support for Lancashire's proposal that the provenance of the play might have been near to Ampthill in Bedfordshire, where Richard Grey, Earl of Kent, had his seat,[65] its author nevertheless could have been imported from nearby Cambridgeshire or even Cambridge itself to provide the play for this patron. The argument for Ampthill is hardly strengthened by the dialect evidence, which does not point to a Bedfordshire location.

The choice of appropriate registers to match characterization is remarkable in the play. Manhode has to go through a series of changes related to his different ages, for example adopting the relatively simple diction of Infans (ll. 28–51) as contrasted with the self-indulgent misery of Age, thick with alliteration (ll. 764–74). There is contrast too between the pompous language of Mundus (ll. 1–14) and the informal impertinence of Folye (ll. 630–34); and even Conscyence is differentiated from Perseveraunce, the one simple and direct (ll. 424–39), the other more self-consciously learned and nearer to a preaching mode (ll. 907–14). While these characteristics may have had a realistic effect, giving a "local habitation" to the demands of allegory, it seems that the differences of the individual voices may have been of particular value as part of the staging. Since there may have been only two actors, it was essential that each character should make a distinctive impact within a very few words of his entrance—a process which could have been enhanced by the symbolism of costume and properties. We should note too that where they address the audience, characters adopt different modes according to whether they are to be respectful, over-friendly, or condescending.

The versification of *The Worlde and the Chylde* has caused some adverse comment in the past: Chamberlin called it a "hodgepodge."[66] We propose, however, that there is a rationale which may explain the two basic choices the author made with some consistency. In general, for serious soliloquies and speeches addressing the audience, he uses quatrains rhyming abab. In contrast, for dialogue, which by definition, in the light of the two-actor doubling adopted here, must be between Manhode in one of his states and a good or bad interlocutor, he chooses tail-rhyme stanzas in the pattern aaabcccb. This may be most clearly seen in the details in Appendix I where the versification structure for the whole play is set out. This broad division into two types of verse may be compared with the procedures in *Mankind* and Medwall's *Nature*. In the former, the villains New Guise, Nowadays, and Nought speak in tail rhyme, while Mercy and Mankind in serious passages usually have quatrains or, in Mercy's case, double concatenated quatrains, making octaves, as in the opening lines. When these two speak to the villains, however, they tend to join into the tail-rhyme. Medwall similarly uses tail-rhyme for informal speeches, with variations between aabccb and aaabcccb. For the more formal passages, however, his chosen contrast is rhyme royal.[67]

In *The Worlde and the Chylde* the distinction between formality and informality is more difficult to make: the tendency is rather that dialogue is in tail-rhyme and soliloquy in quatrains. There are some exceptions: the most interesting is the *tour de force* of Wanton's demonstration of childish games (ll. 77–122). Such distinctions in the use of verse forms, however, may not be determined by such purely rhetorical considerations. There is also the question of the actors' convenience, as well as the need to issue signals to the audience about significance and change. It may well be that in dialogue the presence of plenty of regular rhymes helps the actors to follow cues and to remember lines. Such advantages may arise elsewhere in the case of concatenated rhymes between speeches.

There are however two irregularities to be considered in the proposed scheme. One is that the author does not always offer perfect rhymes, especially in the tail-rhymes. This may be because in places he positively prefers the effect of assonance or approximate rhyme rather than true rhyme and seeks it deliberately. We have the difficulty that shifts in the pronunciation of vowels may have obscured true rhymes, and that which we see in the text as assonance in appearance may indeed not be.[68] For example, wende/frend/mynde (ll. 486–88) was in all probability a true rhyme on /ɛ/. Two important points should be noted: (1) many of the approximate rhymes involve vowels (e.g., ME ē/ī or ō/ū) had recently undergone vowel shifting to become closer to each other than formerly, and (2) the assonating syllables have similar codas—that is, all stops, nasals, or nasal and stop combination.[69] The problem is to decide how far to be sympathetic to the author's "ear." Sometimes we may be tempted to suppose that the text may have been tampered with or perhaps erroneously recorded from something which was initially auditory, but corroborating evidence for such ideas is very hard to find. It is worth noting that in *Mankind* the rhymes are often apparently imperfect.

The second irregularity is perhaps more intriguing: it concerns the places where the author varies from the pattern noted, either by shifting from quatrains to tail-rhymes within the same speech or by interjecting a small number of lines which are themselves bound together by rhyme. Once again Appendix I makes clear where these happen and also the size of interruptions to a regular pattern. The shift usually occurs when a soliloquy is nearing its end, as at line 144. The commonest short stanza is a five-line unit with two rhymes: abbba or some variation based upon a link back to previous rhymes.[70] The purpose of these may be to signal to the audience that some special aspect of meaning is being marked, as in "Shame" at lines 819–23. But again there may also be a benefit to the actors, especially where one is offstage preparing to enter, and a change in rhythm may act as a cue. An example might be Manhode's speech (abbba) before Conscyence's entry at lines 283–87, where the actor playing Conscyence is completing a costume change after his exit as Mundus at line 236. In view of the skill exercised by the author in so many other aspects of this dramatization, we should perhaps accept that these apparent irregularities do have criteria like those mentioned and that they are not therefore examples of incompetence. Further evidence in defense of such a view may be the remarkable way in which he varies the length of lines for different speakers and circumstances. In this way he sometimes creates a rhythm which might be suitable for song, as in Manhode's self-satisfaction at ll. 283–87; whereas at other times the long lines accommodate the learned solemnity of Perseveraunce, as in his "ensaumple" at lines 867–74. Even if the poet is not always consistent or entirely successful in following the strategies described here, it must be proposed that he is a resourceful versifier with a distinctive ear for the sound of verse, a grasp of its potentialities, and a sense of the value of variation in sound.

STAGING. To begin with the historical aspects of staging, we find that the play was most likely presented indoors in the hall of a great house. There are few staging requirements apart from the throne for Mundus. The distinctive voices of the characters were no doubt backed up by costumes, for there is a series of references to costume changes. Then, in the light of the use of the top for Wanton (ll. 78–79) which we have seen echoes the iconographical tradition, other symbolic properties seem quite likely in order to make visual points instantly. There appears to be a such an effect implied by the rich clothing worn by Manhode at his worldly best, where his splendid apparel might rival or imitate that of Mundus. Similarly, the distinctive appearance of Age would be noticeable, and also would have been responsive to iconographical conventions.

The presence of the audience is a marked feature of the text. There are several places where the characters speak directly to them, and in a variety of moods. It does not seem that the text reflects any anxiety about rowdiness. The farewell by Perseveraunce to "kynge and knyght" (l. 974) must raise the possibility that the king was present, but the phrase may only be an alliterative formula. Many of these addresses are in the form of soliloquies in accordance with practices which were established in earlier moralities. On the one hand, these had the function of assisting in the doubling, but there are also subtle and important variations in the way the characters speak—a process which is of fundamental importance to the exploitation of the allegories.

David Bevington has made the justifiable comment that the doubling scheme was arranged with "precision and ingenuity,"[71] but we have set out in Appendix II a possible scheme which makes plain that there are some difficulties which require solutions. As there are never more than two characters on stage, it is reasonable to suppose that the play was designed for two actors, and our scheme is set out accordingly. Such a limited cast is comparatively rare, and the play provides no explanation for it. Yet the two-actor format does not seem to have been a constraint upon what was required from the actors.[72] Though the concept of "professional" actors is hard to define at this period, it does appear that these players would have had a range of skills, and that experience on stage would have been a great help in meeting the speed required for costume changes as well as the variety of roles each actor was required to play.

If we suppose that all the Ages of Manhode must be played by the same actor throughout, the greatest difficulty in the doubling is that it produces the one kind of hitch which is unacceptable if the performance is to be smoothly continuous: the actor playing Conscyence at line 740 must go off and return immediately as Perseveraunce. The solution is to switch roles here, so that the actor who has so far been doing the Manhode roles will now come on as Perseveraunce. When his colleague (Conscyence) reappears some twenty-three lines later he takes the role of Age and plays alongside Perseveraunce until the end of the play. The trappings of Age are such that there would be plenty of ways of suggesting continuity even though a different actor was now involved: it would indeed be a challenge to make a good job of the new disguise.

The second difficulty is perhaps the long periods for which both actors are on stage. Player A as Mundus could have some respite, however, if he were seated in state, while Wanton speaks and performs to the audience in the long and colorful passage which adumbrates children's games (ll. 76–122). Player B has the task of presenting the three younger roles before Manhode emerges. It looks as though the costume changes, and perhaps associated changes of properties, were carried out on stage (as at l. 67), but there is one point at which Mundus has a soliloquy of twenty-one lines (ll. 216–36), where Player B might go off, as his line "now wyll I wende" (l. 214) suggests. In spite of these possible breaks, the scheme is demanding, yet it nevertheless provides an opportunity for the actors to create an engaging variety of theatrical effects. Apparently the author, who may of course have been one of the players, was very experienced in judging the effects which could be achieved, especially in the judicious placing of soliloquies. If the doubling scheme suggested in Appendix II were indeed the one adopted, the play could have run without any hitches.

For a modern production the directness and variety of the language form one of the play's strongest assets. The allegory is apparently a challenge; nevertheless, in spite of the prejudice against this mode, it does in fact work convincingly and engages the audience in an intriguing activity of identification. This level of meaning is especially enhanced by realistic detail, which is, paradoxically, one of the most effective attributes of allegories. It is apparent also that symmetry and contrast in characters and speeches are dramatically attractive.[73] Again it may be possible to call upon iconographic traditions here which are frequently based upon echoic and contrasting principles as in altarpieces in the form of a diptych or a triptych.

PERFORMANCE HISTORY. The effectiveness of the doubling program implied in the text is the strongest evidence that the play was actually produced in the sixteenth century. Quite clearly whoever created the play at least aspired to a production even if one never came about. No external evidence has emerged, however, to prove or disprove the case for a performance. Implicit evidence for a performance rests principally upon the unobtrusive arrangements for doubling and the interest in costume in the dialogue.

The Worlde and the Chylde has had a more extensive stage history throughout the twentieth century than many other early moralities. It attracted the attention of Nugent Monck, who as a young man was stage manager to William Poel in the latter's revival of *Everyman* in 1900. By 1910 Monck had taken up residence in Norwich, and in that year he initiated a series of performances of *The Worlde and the Chylde*, starting in the drawing room of "The Crypt," his house in Bethel Street. Apparently the room was large enough to accommodate an audience of seventy. Subsequently his efforts continued more widely. In Norwich he took the play to Blackfriars (St. Andrew's) Hall in 1910,[74] and to the thatched Assembly Rooms in 1912. Then, because of a link he had forged with William Butler Yeats, he arranged a performance of the play on 29 February and 2 March in that year at the Abbey Theatre in Dublin. On this occasion he used acting students for most of the parts but played Manhood himself—a sign that he did not follow the doubling which is implicit in the structure of the play. The commentator thought the production was "beautifully staged and impressively acted," and drew attention to skillful use of color, lighting, and grouping.[75] Sometimes Monck's productions were associated with *Youth* or with a version of the St. George play. On 3 July 1913 his company, now the Norwich Players, performed *The Worlde and the Chylde* at Lambeth Palace in the presence of the Archbishop of Canterbury and the Bishop of London.[76] Though the Players were dispersed during World War I, Monck returned to *The Worlde and the Chylde* when a new phase opened in their reconstitution in 1919. They now acquired a new theater at the Old Music House, in King Street, Norwich, where the play was again presented in 1920. In the following year Monck led his company into their new Maddermarket Theatre, but the published lists of the repertoire do not show that *The Worlde and the Chylde* was ever presented in that remarkable auditorium. June Ottaway commented that Monck's "work is characterized by simplicity, directness, artistic integrity and a conspicuous absence of misplaced reverence."[77]

After World War II, *The Worlde and the Chylde* was revived in a newly developing academic environment. It was produced at the University of Chicago in the late 1960s by Annette Fern. This occasion was remarkable in that only two actors doubled all the parts, a procedure which emphasizes the extent to which two such actors have enormous scope for their versatile acting skills. This choice also has possible implications about the interplay of characterization as it plays on the links between Mundus and Folye.

The Poculi Ludique Societas of the University of Toronto performed the play, with musical additions, in the context of their many other medieval revivals in the 1978–79 season. "Mankind" was played by John Mayberry; World, doubled with Perseveraunce by Allan Park; and Conscyence, doubled with Folly by Jonathan Pearl. In her program notes Kathy Pearl, the director, called attention to the "beauty of language and the sympathetic understanding of human nature." Influenced by Lancashire's suggested historical context, she noted the interplay between "typical allegorical characters and those who, masked under the façade of allegory, may have had counterparts in [Richard] Grey's life" (see fig. 16). Another PLS production was mounted in 1979 when the play was done at Indiana University on 18 October with David Parry as Conscyence and K. Reed Needles as Folye.[78] There was a further performance at the Société Internationale pour l'Etude du Théâtre Médiéval colloquium at University College, Dublin, in July 1980.[79]

EDITIONS. The earliest modern text of *The Worlde and the Chylde* was the typographical facsimile prepared in 1817 for the Roxburghe Club from the 1522 quarto when it was temporarily in the hands of John Charles Spencer, Lord Althorp.[80] This edition, of which only thirty-four copies were printed, would in turn be used by John M. Manly in preparing the text included in volume 1 of his *Specimens of the Pre-Shaksperean Drama* (1897). In the meantime, a modern-spelling version of the play had been included by Collier in the third edition of Dodsley's *A Select Collection of Old English Plays* (1825), and it was retained by W. Carew Hazlitt in the fourth edition (1874). None of these editions contains critical notes, nor of course does John S. Farmer's facsimile, which was issued in the Tudor Facsimile Texts series. Since there are only rudimentary notes in Farmer's *Six Anonymous Plays: First Series* (1905), the only previous edition with full critical apparatus is the dissertation by Mallory Chamberlin, Jr., in 1969. Two classroom collections, by Edgar T. Schell and J. D. Schuchter (*English Morality Plays and Moral Interludes*) and by G. A. Lester (*Three Late Medieval Morality Plays*), present modern-spelling texts.

EDITORIAL PRINCIPLES. The present edition of *The Worlde and the Chylde* is based upon the quarto in the library of Trinity College, Dublin. Old spelling has been retained, and all emendations have been noted in the textual apparatus. Abbreviations have been expanded and appear in italics. Punctuation has been added throughout to make the text more accessible to modern readers. The original printing took no account of the stanzaic structures, and these have been supplied for the present edition (see Appendix I).

NOTES

[1] The term 'morality' was not current in medieval times but was adopted as late as the eighteenth century; see Robert Potter, *The English Morality Play* (London: Routledge and Kegan Paul, 1975), 6–7, and David Mills, *Re-Cycling the Cycle: The City of Chester and Its Whitsun Plays* (Toronto: University of Toronto Press, 1998), 7.

[2] Pamela Sheingorn, "On Using Medieval Art in the Study of Medieval Drama: An Introduction to Methodology," *Research Opportunities in Renaissance Drama* 22 (1979): 101–09; see also Graham Runnalls, "Were They Listening or Watching? Text and Spectacle at the 1510 Châteaudun *Passion Play*," *Medieval English Theatre* 16 (1994): 25.

[3] See Eamon Duffy, *The Stripping of the Altars* (New Haven: Yale University Press, 1992).

[4] W. W. Greg, *A Bibliography of the English Printed Drama to the Restoration*, 4 vols. (London: Bibliographical Society, 1939), 1:81–85. For the facsimile, see James S. Farmer, ed., *The World and the Chylde*, Tudor Facsimile Texts (Edinburgh and London: T. C. and E. C. Jack, 1909). The facsmile was reprinted by AMS Press in 1970.

[5] Ibid., nos. 3, 7, 20a; see *Two Tudor Interludes: Youth and Hickscorner*, ed. Ian Lancashire (Manchester: Manchester University Press, 1980).

[6] F. Madan, "Day-Book of John Dorne, Bookseller in Oxford, A.D. 1520," *Collectanea*, I, ed. C. R. L. Fletcher (Oxford: Oxford Historical Society, 1885), 130. For discussion of the history of the Trinity College, Dublin, copy, see Ian Lancashire, "The Provenance of *The Worlde and the Chylde*," *Papers of the Bibliographical Society of America* 67 (1973): 377–88.

[7] Other works that may be included in this list and which are earlier include the *Speculum Humanae Salvationis* and the *Biblia Pauperum*; for the latter see Avril Henry, ed., *Biblia Pauperum* (Aldershot: Scolar Press, 1987). See also the devotional readings surveyed by Duffy, *The Stripping of the Altars*, 233–65.

[8] Ian Lancashire, "The Auspices of *The World and the Child*," *Renaissance and Reformation* 12 (1976): 96–105.

[9] For the use of woodcuts by Wynkyn de Worde's press, see Martha Driver, "The Illustrated de Worde: An Overview," *Studies in Iconography* 17 (1996): 349–403.

[10] Edward Hodnett, *English Woodcuts, 1480–1535* (Oxford: Oxford University Press, 1973), no. 336. The woodcut, much more worn, would appear again as late as c.1585; see *The Kalender of Sheephards (c. 1585)*, introd. S. K. Heninger (Delmar, N.Y.: Scholars' Facsimiles and Reprints, 1979), 111.

[11] Lancashire, "The Auspices of *The World and the Child*," 97.

[12] See the arguments of Suzanne Westfall for household performance of the play in her *Patrons and Performance: Early Tudor Revels* (Oxford: Clarendon Press, 1990), 172, 190.

[13] T. W. Craik, *The Tudor Interlude: Stage, Costume, and Acting* (Leicester: Leicester University Press, 1958), 140.

[14] See *DNB, s.v.* Edmund Dudley, Richard Empson.

[15] Lancashire, "The Auspices of *The World and the Child*," 97–98.

[16] Edward H. Sugden, *A Topographical Dictionary to the Works of Shakespeare and His Fellow Dramatists* (Manchester, 1925), 291.

[17] See *The Castle of Perseverance*, ll. 170–82, in *The Macro Plays*, ed. Mark Eccles, EETS, o.s 262 (London: Oxford University Press, 1968); Stephen Spector, ed., *The N-Town Play*, EETS, s.s. 10–11 (Oxford: Oxford University Press, 1991), 2:485.

[18] Lancashire, "The Auspices of *The World and the Child*," 99, n. 26.

[19] Henry Noble MacCracken, "A Source of *Mundus et Infans*," *PMLA* 23 (1909): 486–96. For the poem, see *Hymns to the Virgin and Christ, the Parliament of Devils, and Other Religious Poems*, ed. Frederick J. Furnivall, EETS, o.s. 24 (1868; reprint New York: Greenwood Press, 1969), 58–78. See also Ernest G. York, "The Mirror of the Periods of Man's Life," unpublished diss. (University of Pennsylvania, 1957).

[20] Compare *The Mirror*, ll. 4, 6, with *The Worlde and the Chylde*, ll. 31, 35.

[21] The term 'Lykynge' is of special interest since it is used in John Trevisa's translation of the *De Proprietatibus Rerum* in connection with children's activities; see Bartholomaeus

Anglicus, *On the Properties of Things*, trans. John Trevisa, ed. M. C. Seymour et al., 3 vols. (Oxford: Clarendon Press, 1975–78), 1:292.

[22] MacCracken, "A Source of *Mundus et Infans*," 494; compare *The Mirror*, ll. 541–42, with *The Worlde and the Chylde*, ll. 859–64.

[23] See Morton W. Bloomfield, *The Seven Deadly Sins* (East Lansing: Michigan State College Press, 1952), passim.

[24] These are the Three Enemies of Man, a commonplace of late medieval iconography; see Samuel Chew, *The Pilgrimage of Life* (New Haven: Yale University Press, 1962), 70–78, and Siegfried Wenzel, "The Three Enemies of Man," *Mediaeval Studies* 29 (1967): 47–66. The presence of the World as one of the Three Enemies is important for *The Worlde and the Chylde*, for Mundus must be identified with the World that is renounced, along with the Devil and all his pomps, in the rite of baptism; see Henry Ansgar Kelly, *The Devil at Baptism: Ritual, Theology, and Drama* (Ithaca: Cornell University Press, 1985), 97–102.

[25] See Roberta D. Cornelius, *The Figurative Castle* (Bryn Mawr, 1930), 16–17, and Cornelius's edition, "*Le Songe du Castel*," *PMLA* 46 (1931): 321–32.

[26] Alan H. Nelson, "*Of the seuen ages*: An Unknown Analogue of *The Castle of Perseverance*," *Comparative Drama* 8 (1974): 125–38. See also R. H. Bowers, "A Medieval Analogue to *As You Like It* II.vii.137–166," *Shakespeare Quarterly* 3 (1952): 109–12; Ernest C. York, "Dramatic Form in a Late Medieval English Narrative," *Modern Language Notes* 72 (1957): 484–85; and the discussion in Clifford Davidson, *Visualizing the Moral Life: Medieval Iconography and the Macro Moralities* (New York: AMS Press, 1989), 54–56.

[27] *The Macro Plays*, ed. Eccles; Thomas Chaundler, *Liber Apologeticus de Omni Statu Humanae Naturae: A Defense of Nature in Every State (c.1460)*, ed. Doris Enright-Clark Shoukri, Publications of the Modern Humanities Research Institute, 5 (London, 1974).

[28] *Non-Cycle Plays and Fragments*, ed. Norman Davis, EETS, s.s. 1 (London: Oxford University Press, 1970), lxxxvi, 90–106, pl. III.

[29] Henry Medwall, *The Plays*, ed. Alan H. Nelson (Cambridge: D. S. Brewer, 1980); John Skelton, *Magnificence*, ed. Paula Neuss (Manchester: Manchester University Press, 1980).

[30] The following *Records of Early English Drama* volumes have been published to date: York; Chester; Coventry; Newcastle; Norwich (1540–1642); Devon; Shropshire; Cumberland, Westmorland, and Gloucestershire; Herefordshire and Worcestershire; Somerset; Lancashire; Bristol; and Dorset and Cornwall. See also Westfall, *Patrons of Performance*, and Alexandra F. Johnston and Wim Hüsken, eds., *English Parish Drama* (Amsterdam: Rodopi, 1996). For plays in the great hall tradition, see Greg Walker, *The Politics of Performance in Early Renaissance Drama* (Cambridge: Cambridge University Press, 1998), 232–36.

[31] See pp. 23–25, below, and Appendix II. For another view, incorporating a boy actor, see Richard Southern, *The Staging of Plays before Shakespeare* (London: Faber and Faber, 1973), 135.

[32] In the fifteenth-century *moralité L'Omme Pecheur*, Raison and other virtuous characters lead L'Omme to Monde because, like Adam after the Fall, he is born to labor; see

Werner Helmich, ed., *Moralités Françaises* (Geneva: Slatkine, 1980), 157.

[33] See Potter, *The English Morality Play*, 46.

[34] See David Mills, "Anglo-Dutch Theatres: Problems and Possibilities," *Medieval English Theatre* 18 (1996): 85–98.

[35] Samuel Taylor Coleridge, *The Complete Works*, ed. W. G. T. Shedd, 7 vols. (New York: Harper, 1884), 1:437–38.

[36] See Davidson, *Visualizing the Moral Life*, 6–8, and Paul Piehler, *The Visionary Landscape* (London: Edward Arnold, 1971), 11.

[37] Gay Clifford, *The Transformations of Allegory* (London: Routledge and Kegan Paul, 1984), 14.

[38] For further discussion, see Peter Happé, "Dramatic Images of Kingship in Heywood and Bale," *SEL: Studies in English Literature* 39 (1999): 239–53, and "Allegorical Kings as staged by Skelton and Lindsay," *Theta* 5 (forthcoming).

[39] Elizabeth Sears, *The Ages of Man: Medieval Interpretations of the Life Cycle* (Princeton: Princeton University Press, 1986), passim.

[40] Adolf Katzenellenbogen, *Allegories of the Virtues and Vices in Mediaeval Art*, trans. Alan J. P. Crick (London: Warburg Institute, 1939), 72, esp. n. 3.

[41] Mallory Chamberlin, Jr., "The World and the Child, Otherwise Called *Mundus et Infans*," Ph.D. diss., University of Tennessee (1969), 13.

[42] For the now underestimated popularity of Barclay's work, see Robert C. Evans, "Forgotten Fools: Alexander Barclay's *Ship of Fools*," and, for theatrical aspects, Peter Happé, "Staging Folly in the Early Sixteenth Century: Heywood, Lindsay, and Others," in *Fools and Folly*, ed. Clifford Davidson, Early Drama, Art, and Music, Monograph Series, 22 (Kalamazoo: Medieval Institute Publications, 1996), 47–72 and 73–111. Some useful notes on the background of the fool are presented in D. J. Gifford, "Iconographical Notes toward a Definition of the Medieval Fool," *Journal of the Warburg and Courtauld Institutes* 37 (1974): 336–37; for extended discussion, see Enid Welsford, *The Fool* (London: Faber and Faber, 1935); and Sandra Billington, *A Social History of the Fool* (Brighton: Harvester, 1984). See also Peter Happé, "Fansy and Foly: The Drama of Fools in *Magnyfycence*," *Comparative Drama* 27 (1993–94): 426–52.

[43] For ways in which Folye anticipates the development of the Vice, see David M. Bevington, *From* Mankind *to* Marlowe (Cambridge: Harvard University Press, 1962), 122–23.

[44] For a description of Augustine's schema as presented in *De Genesi contra Manichaeos* which had also correlated the Ages of Man with the Ages of the World, see Paul Archambault, "The Ages of Man and the Ages of the World," *Revue des Études Augustiniennes* 12 (1966): 203–05; for Isidore of Seville, see his *Etymologia*, ed. W. M. Lindsay, 2 vols. (Oxford: Clarendon Press, 1911), XI.ii.1–8; and for Aquinas, see his Commentary on Hebrews, as quoted in M.-D. Chenu, *Nature, Man, and Society in the Twelfth Century*, trans. Jerome Taylor and Lester K. Little (Chicago: University of Chicago Press, 1968), 183. See also Sears, *The Ages of Man*, 61, 123, 197; J. A. Burrow, *The Ages of Man: A Study in*

Medieval Writing and Thought (Oxford: Clarendon Press, 1986), 82–83, 85–86; and, for an early study, John Winter Jones, "Observations on the Origin of the Division of Man's Life into Stages," *Archaeologia* 35 (1853): 167–89.

[45] Isidore of Seville, *Etymologia*, XI.ii.1–8, as quoted in translation by Sears, *The Ages of Man*, 61.

[46] *Promptorium Parvulorum*. ed. A. L. Mayhew, EETS, e.s. 102 (London, 1908), 7 (*s.v.* "agis sevyn").

[47] Madeline Caviness, *The Windows of Christ Church Cathedral, Canterbury*, Corpus Vitrearum Medii Aevi, 2 (London: Royal Academy, 1981), 110–11, figs. 181, 186, 187a. The inscriptions identify the six figures as ranging from INFANTIA to SENECTUS, the latter represented as an old man with a walking stick. PVERITIA has a ball and stick for playing a children's game, while IVVENTVS carries the sword. The heads now in this glass are all modern replacements except for Infantia.

[48] See ibid. and, for further discussion, Archambault, "The Ages of Man and the Ages of the World," 193–228.

[49] See M. R. James, "*Pictor in Carmine*," *Archaeologia* 94 (1951): 155, under the heading "Mutat Christus aquam in uinum": "Tropolgica intelligentia de sex ydriis per sex gradus etatis humane."

[50] Facsimile in H. Oskar Sommer, *The Kalender of Shepherdes*, 3 vols. (London: Kegan Paul, Trench, Trübner, 1892), 2:L4ᵛ–L5ᵛ. This early translation of the French text of *Le Kalendrier et Compost des Bergiers* was printed at Paris by Antoine Vérard under the title *The Kalendayr of the Shyppars* and was in rather garbled English. Pynson published a corrected prose summary of the Ages of Man section in 1506 (see Sommer, 3:152–53), and Robert Copland's translation of the verse appeared in the edition issued by Wynkyn de Worde, *The Kalender of shepeherdes* (London, 1508). See the discussion of the various editions in Sommer, 1:11–98, and Erik Dal and Povl Skårup, *The Ages of Man and the Months of the Year* (Copenhagen: Munksgaard, 1980), 20–25.

[51] Dal and Skårup, *The Ages of Man and the Months of the Year*, figs. 44–46.

[52] There is a recovery of wealth in October, followed by sickness in November and a deathbed scene in December; see ibid., figs. 49, 52, 55.

[53] See Audrey Baker, "The Interpretation and Iconography of the Longthorpe Paintings," *Archaeologia* 96 (1955): 43–44; E. W. Tristram, *English Wall Painting of the Fourteenth Century* (London: Routledge and Kegan Paul, 1955), 219. For a Continental example which also preserves the arch structure of the Ages of Man, see the woodcut by J. Breu the Younger, who illustrates them as ten figures on an arched bridge; above the man at the highest point on the bridge is Death with his bow, while below the final step on the bridge is a niche with a bier representing the final stage of life; see Max Geisberg, *The German Single-Leaf Woodcut, 1500–1550*, ed. Walter L. Strauss, 4 vols. (New York: Hacker, 1974), no. G.401.

[54] This commonplace is also stressed in a fifteenth-century poem where the high point of the arch is like noontime in the day, after which one goes "all dounward witt þe hylle" (*Religious Lyrics of the XVth Century*, ed. Carleton Brown [Oxford: Clarendon Press, 1939], no. 147).

[55] The accompanying text in the *Omne Bonum* is derived from Bartholomaeus Anglicus's *De Proprietatibus Rerum*; see Lucy Freeman Sandler, *Omne Bonum: A Fourteenth-Century Encyclopedia of Universal Knowledge*, 2 vols. (London: Harvey Miller, 1996), 2:176. See also Sears, *The Ages of Man*, 126, fig. 67. A childe *"playing at the top and squyrge"* (i.e., with a whip top) appeared in the Four Ages scene on tapestries in the house of Thomas More where the next panel identified the *"freshe yonge man"* as "Manhod" (Thomas More, *The English Works*, 2 vols. [London: Eyre and Spottiswoode, 1931], 1: 332–33); this example is cited by Chew, *The Pilgrimage of Life*, 157–58. The Four Ages were conventionally held to correspond with the humors, as follows: child—phlegm (cold, moist); youth—sanguine (hot, moist); man—yellow bile (warm-dry); old—black bile (cold, dry); see Sears, *The Ages of Man*, 25–31, and Raymond Klibansky, Erwin Panofsky, and Fritz Saxl, *Saturn and Melancholy* (London: Thomas Nelson, 1964), 292–97.

[56] Sears, *The Ages of Man*, fig. 67.

[57] For another example of the Wheel, see Gordon McN. Rushforth, "The Wheel of the Ten Ages of Life in Leominster Church," *Proceedings of the Society of Antiquaries* 26 (1914): 47–60, esp. 51–55.

[58] On the two types of despair, one leading, as in the case of Augustine, to conversion and ultimately to salvation, and the other to damnation, see Susan Snyder, "The Left Hand of God: Despair in Medieval and Renaissance Tradition," *Renaissance Studies* 12 (1965): 18–59.

[59] For the woodcut in Brant's *Das Narrenschiff*, see Chew, *The Pilgrimage of Life*, fig. 63, and for the copy of it in Barclay's translation, see sig. 11ᵛ in Pynson's bilingual edition of 1509 and in *The Shyppe of Fooles* (Wynkyn de Worde, 1517), fol. 77.

[60] See Clifford Davidson, *The Guild Chapel Wall Paintings at Stratford-upon-Avon* (New York: AMS Press, 1988), 34, 54; cf. *The Dance of Death*, ed. Florence Warren, EETS, o.s. 181 (London: Oxford University Press, 1931), 74.

[61] Kathleen Cohen, *The Metamorphosis of a Death Symbol: The Transi Tomb in the Late Middle Ages and the Renaissance* (Berkeley and Los Angeles: University of California Press, 1973), fig. 13.

[62] See the discussion in Clifford Davidson, *Illustrations of the Stage and Acting in England to 1580*, Early Drama, Art, and Music, Monograph Series, 16 (Kalamazoo: Medieval Institute Publications, 1991), 67–75.

[63] On costuming for the fool in the later sixteenth century, see Leslie Hotson, *Shakespeare's Motley* (London: Hart-Davies, 1952), esp. 1–15, but also the remarks in Craik, *The Tudor Interlude*, 67–68.

[64] See Angus McIntosh, Michael L. Samuels, and Michael Benskin, *Linguistic Atlas of Later Medieval English*, 4 vols. (Aberdeen: Aberdeen University Press, 1986).

[65] Lancashire, "The Auspices of *The World and the Child*," 100–02.

[66] Chamberlin, "The World and the Child," 77.

[67] Medwall, *The Plays*, ed. Nelson, 26.

[68] For example, a rather distant assonance is found in yprobyde/ipyght/belouyd (ll. 216–18); and it is difficult to know now how close in sound were frere/here/fyre (ll. 400–02). For discussion of the rhymes as dialect evidence, see Appendix III.

[69] For these points we are grateful to Paul A. Johnston, Jr. See also Appendix III.

[70] See the right-hand column in Appendix I, where the five-line abbba and its close variants are apparent.

[71] Bevington, *From* Mankind *to Marlowe*, 116–17. Bevington fitted *The Worlde and the Chylde* into his thesis about the way doubling furthered the process of compression and alternation necessitated by the small size of acting troupes in the sixteenth century; he considered the play a "landmark" in the process (124).

[72] John Bale's *God's Promises* (c.1538) was also constructed for two players, one of whom was apparently Bale himself.

[73] See Bevington, *From* Mankind *to Marlowe*, 119.

[74] Briefly noticed in *The Eastern Daily Press*, 23 December 1910, 5.

[75] *The Irish Times*, 1 March, 1912, 5. The writer praised the acting of Felix Hughes, a "clever youngster" who played the Child.

[76] The note in *The Times* of 4 July 1913, 11, is more concerned to list the grandees present than to describe the performance.

[77] June Ottaway, "Nugent Monck of Norwich," *Christian Drama* 2 (1953): 21–23. For Monck's work, see also Harold Child, "Revivals of English Dramatic Works, 1919–1925," *Review of English Studies* 2 (1926): 177–80; T. L. G. Burley, *Playhouses and Players of East Anglia* (Norwich: Eastern Daily Press, 1928), 94–103; Andrew Stephenson, *The Maddermarket Theatre* (Norwich: The Norwich Players, 1971).

[78] Reviewed by Kay R. Sloan in *Research Opportunities in Renaissance Drama* 22 (1979): 141–42.

[79] *Research Opportunities in Renaissance Drama* 23 (1980): 86.

[80] Lord Spencer had purchased *The Worlde and the Chylde* from Longman's, a London bookseller, who in turn had acquired it as part of a set of books stolen from the library of Trinity College, Dublin. The copy of *The Worlde and the Chylde* was thereafter returned to Trinity College; see the account of this episode in Lancashire, "The Provenance of *The Worlde and the Chylde*," 377–88.

Here begynneth

A Propre Newe Interlude
of The Worlde and the Chylde,

Otherwyse Called

Mundus *et* Infans

And it sheweth of the estate of Chyldehode
and Manhode

MUNDUS

Syrs, seace of your sawes what so befall
And loke ye bow bonerly to my byddyng,
For I am ruler of realmes I warne you all
And ouer all fodys I am kynge,

For I am kynge and well knowen in these realmes rounde.   5
I haue also paleys ypyght,
I haue stedes in stable stalworthe and stronge,
Also stretes and strondes full strongely ydyght,

For all the Worlde Wyde, I wote well, is my name.
All rychesse redely it renneth in me,   10
All pleasure worldely, bothe myrthe and game.
Myselfe semely in sale I sende with you to be,

For I am the Worlde, I warne you all,
Prynce of powere and of plente.
He that cometh not whan I do hym call   15
I shall hym smyte with pouerte,

35

For pouerte I parte in many a place
To them that wyll not obedyent be.
I am a kynge in euery case.
Me thynketh I am a god of grace;   20

The floure of vertu foloweth me.
Lo, here I sette semely in se.
I commaunde you all obedyent be
And with fre wyll ye folowe me.

                                                    [*Enter Infans*
                         INFANS
Cryst our kynge, grau*n*te you clerly to know þe case,   25
To meue of this mater that is in my mynde.
Clerely declare it, Cryst graunte me grace.

Now semely syrs, beholde on me
How mankynde doth begynne.
I am a chylde, as you may se,   30
Goten in game and in grete synne.

Forty wekes my moder me founde,   Aii
Fles<sh>e and blode my fode was tho.
Whan I was rype from her to founde
In peryll of dethe we stode bothe two.   35

Now to seke dethe I must begyn
For to passe that strayte passage,
For body and soule that shall than twynne
And make a partynge of that maryage.

Fourty wekes I was frely fedde   40
Within my moders possessyon.
Full oft of dethe she was adred
Whan that I sholde parte her from.

Now in to the worlde she hathe me sent,
Poore and naked as ye may se.   45

I am not worthely wrapped nor went
But powerly prycked in pouerte.

Now in to the Worlde wyll I wende
Some comforte of hym for to craue.
All hayle, comely crowned kynge,　　　　　　50
God that all made, you se and saue.

MUNDUS

Welcome, fayre chylde, <u>what is thy name</u>?

INFANS

I wote not, syr, withouten blame,
But ofte tyme my moder in her game
　　　<u>Called me Dalyaunce</u>.　　　　　　55

MUNDUS

Dalyaunce, my swete chylde,
It is a name that is ryght wylde,
For whan thou waxest olde
　　　It is a name of no substaunce.

But, my fayre chylde, what woldest thou haue?　　60

INFANS

Syr, of some comforte I you craue,
Mete and clothe my lyfe to saue,
　　　And I your true seruaunt shall be.　　　　[Aii^v]

MUNDUS

Now fayre chylde, I graunte the thyne askynge.
I wyll the fynde whyle thou art yinge　　　　65
So thou wylte be obedyent to my byddynge.
　　　These garmentes gaye I gyue to the,
And also I gyue to the a name
<u>And clepe the Wanton in euery game</u>
Tyll fourteen yere be come and gone,　　　　70

And than come agayne to me.

WANTON

Gramercy, Worlde, for myne araye,
For now I purpose me to playe.

MUNDUS

Fare well, fayre chylde, and haue good daye.
    All rychelesnesse is kynde for the.   75

WANTON

A ha, Wanton is my name.
I can many a quaynte game.
Lo, my toppe I dryue in same.
    Se, it torneth rounde.
I can with my scorge stycke   80
My felowe vpon the heed hytte
And wyghtly from hym make a skyppe
    And blere on hym my tonge.

If brother or syster do me chyde
I wyll scratche and also byte.   85
I can crye and also kyke
    And mocke them all be rewe.
If fader or mother wyll me smyte
I wyll wrynge with my lyppe
And lyghtly from hym make a skyppe   90
    And call my dame shrewe.

A ha, a newe game haue I founde.
Se this gynne, it renneth rounde.   Aiii
And here another haue I founde,
    And yet mo can I fynde.   95
I can mowe on a man,
And make a lesynge well I can
And mayntayne it ryght well than.
    This connynge came me of kynde.

Ye, syrs, I can well gelde a snayle 100
And catche a cowe by the tayle
   This is a fayre connynge.
I can daunce and also skyppe,
I can playe at the chery pytte,
And I can wystell you a fytte, 105
   Syres, in a whylowe ryne.

Ye, syrs, and euery daye
Whan I to scole shall take the waye
Some good mannes gardyn I wyll assaye,
   Perys and plommes to plucke. 110
I can spye a sparowes nest.
I wyll not go to scole but whan me lest,
For there begynneth a sory fest
   Whan the mayster sholde lyfte my docke.

But, syrs, whan I was seu<e>n yere of age 115
I was sent to the Worlde to take wage,
And this seuen yere I haue ben his page
   And kept his commaundement.
Now I wyll wende to the Worlde, þe worthy emperou<r>.
Hayle, lorde of grete honour, 120
This seuen yere I haue serued you in hall *and* in boure
   With all my trewe entent.

MUNDUS

Now welcome, Wanton, my derlynge dere.
A newe name I shall gyue the here:
Loue, Lust, Lykynge in fere. 125
   These thy names they shall be, [Aiii^v]
All game and gle and gladnes,
All loue longynge in lewdnes.
This seuen yere forsake all sadnes
   And than come agayne to me. 130

LUST *AND* LYKYNGE

A ha, now Lust and Lykynge is my name.
I am as fresshe as flourys in Maye.
I am semely shapen in same
And proudely apperelde in garmentes gaye.

My lokes ben full louely to a ladyes eye,   135
And in loue longynge my harte is sore sette.
Myght I fynde a fode that were fayre and fre.
To lye in hell tell domysdaye for loue I wolde not let

My loue for to wynne.
All game and gle,   140
All myrthe and melodye,
All reuell and ryotte,
And of bost wyll I neuer blynne.

But syrs, now I am nineteen wynter olde.
Iwys, I waxe wonder bolde.   145
Now I wyll go to the Worlde
     A heygher scyence to assaye.
For the Worlde wyll me auaunce,
I wyll kepe his gouernaunce.
For he is a kynge in all substaunce,   150
     His plesynge wyll I praye.

All hayle, mayster, full of myght.
I haue you serued bothe day and nyght.
Now I comen as I you behyght;
     One and twenty wynter is comen and gone.   155

MUNDUS

Now welcome, Loue, Lust, and Lykynge.
For thou hast ben obedyent to my byddynge
I encrease the in all thynge   [Aiiii]
     And myghtly I make the a man.

Manhode myghty shall be thy name. 160
Bere the prest in euery game,
And wayte well that thou suffre no shame
    Neyther for londe nor for rente.
Yf ony man wolde wayte the with blame,
Withstonde hym with thy hole entent. 165
Full sharpely thou bete hym to shame
    With doughtynesse of dede.

For of one thynge, Manhode, I warne the:
I am moost of bounte,
For seuen kynges sewen me 170
    Bothe by daye and nyght.
One of them is the kynge of Pryde;
The kynge of Enuy, doughty in dede;
The kynge of Wrathe, that boldely wyll abyde
    For mykyll is his myght. 175

The kynge of Couetous is the fourte.
The fyfte kynge he hyght Slouthe.
The kynge of Glotony hath no iolyte
    There Pouerte is pyght.
Lechery is the seuenth kynge, 180
All men in hym haue grete delytynge;
Therfore worshyp hym aboue all thynge,
    Manhode, with all thy myght.

MANHODE

Yes, syr kynge, without lesynge
It shall be wrought. 185
Had I knowynge of the fyrst kynge without lesynge,
    Well oyen I mought.

MUNDUS

The fyrste kynge hyght Pryde.

MANHODE

A lorde, with hym fayne wolde I byde.   [Aiiii^v]

MUNDUS

Ye, but woldest thou serue hym truely in euery tyde?   190

MANHODE

Ye, syr, and therto my trouthe I plyght.

That I shall truely Pryde present
I swere by Saynt Thomas of Kent.
To serue hym truely is myn entent
        With mayne and all my myght.   195

MUNDUS

Now Manhode, I wyll araye the newe
In robes ryall, ryght of good hewe.
And I praye the pryncypally be trewe,
        And here I dubbe the a knyght,
And haunte alwaye to chyualry.   200
I gyue the grace and also beaute,
Golde and syluer, grete plente
        Of the wronge to make the ryght.

MANHODE

Gramercy, Worlde and emperour.
Gramercy, Worlde and gouernoure.   205
Gramercy, comforte in all coloure.
        And now I take my leue; fare well.

MUNDUS

Farewell, Manhode, my gentyll knyght.
Fare well, my sone, semely in syght.
I gyue the a swerde *and* also strength and myght   210
        In batayle boldly to bere the well.

MANHODE

Now I am dubbed a knyght hende.
Wonder wyde shall waxe my fame.
To seke aduentures now wyll I wende
    To please the Worlde in gle and game. 215

MUNDUS

Lo, syrs, I am a prynce, peryllous yprobyde, [Av]
Ipreuyd full peryllous and pethely ipyght
As a lorde in eche londe I am belouyd.
Myne eyen do shyne as lanterne bryght.

I am a creature comely out of care. 220
Emperours and kynges they knele to my kne.
Euery man is aferde whan I do on hym stare,
For all mery medell erthe maketh mencyon of me.

Yet all is at my hande werke, both by downe *and* by dale,
Bothe the see and the lande and foules that fly. 225
And I were ones moued, I tell you in tale,
There durst no sterre stere that stondeth in the sky,

For I am lorde and leder so that in londe.
All boweth to my byddynge bonerly aboute.
Who þat styreth w*ith* ony stryfe or wayteth me with wro*n*ge, 230
I shall myghtly make hym to stamer *and* stowpe,

For I am rychest in myne araye.
I haue knyghtes and toures.
I haue ladyes bryghtest in bourys.
Now wyll I fare on these flourys. 235
    Lordynges, haue good daye. [*Exit*

MANHODE

Peas, now peas, ye felowes all aboute.
Peas now and herken to my sawes,
For I am lorde bothe stalworthy and stowte.

All londes are ledde by my lawes.   240

Baron was there neuer borne that so well hym bare,
A better ne a bolder nor a bryghter of ble.
For I haue myght *and* mayne ouer countrees fare,
And Manhode myghty am I named in euery cou*n*tre,

For Salerne and Samers and Ynde the Loys,   245
Caleys, Kente, *and* Cornewayle I haue conquered clene,
Pycardye and Pountes and gentyll Artoys,
Florence, Flaunders, and Frau*n*ce, *and* also Gascoyne.

All I haue conquered as a knyght.   [Av^v]
There is no emperour so kene   250
That dare me lyghtly tene,
For lyues and lymmes I lene,
    So mykyll is my myght.

For I haue boldely blode full pyteously dyspylde,
There many hath lefte fyngers *and* fete, both heed *and* face. 255
I haue done harme on hedes *and* knyghtes haue I kyld,
And many a lady for my loue hath sayd alas.

Brygaunt Ernys I haue beten to backe *and* to bonys,
And beten also many a grome to grounde.
Brestplates I haue beten as Steuen was w*ith* stonys;   260
So fell a fyghter in a felde was there neuer yfounde.

To me no man is makyde,
For Manhode myghty, that is my name.
Many a lorde haue I do lame.
Wonder wyde walketh my fame,   265
    And many a kynges crowne haue I crakyd.

I am worthy and wyght, wytty and wyse.
I am ryall arayde to reuen vnder the ryse.
I am proudely aparelde in purpure and byse.
    As golde I glyster in gere.   270

I am styffe, stronge, stalworthe, and stoute.
I am the ryallest redely that renneth in this route.
There is no knyght so grysly that I drede nor dout,
    For I am so doughtly dyght ther may no dint me dere.

And þe kynge of Pryde, full prest, with all his proude presens, 275
And þe kynge of Lechery louely his letters hath me sent,
And the kynge of Wrathe full wordely, with all his entent
    They wyll me mayntayne with mayne *and* all theyr myght.
The kynge of Couetous and the kynge of Glotony,
The kynge of Slouthe and the kynge of Enuy 280
All those sende me theyr leuery.
    Where is now so worthy a wyght?

A wyght, [Avi]
Ye, as a wyght wytty
Here in this sete sytte I, 285
For no loues lette I
    Here for to sytte.

                [*Enter Conscyence*

CONSCYENCE

Cryst, as he is crowned kynge,
Saue all this comely company
And graunte you all his dere blessynge 290
That bonerly bought you on the roode tre.

Now praye you prestly on euery syde
To God omnypotent
To set our enemy sharpely on syde —
That is, the deuyll and his couent — 295

And all men to haue a clere knowynge
Of heuen blysse, that hye toure.
Me thynke it is a nessarye thynge
For yonge and olde, bothe ryche and pore

Poore Conscyence for to knowe,   300
For Conscyence clere it is my name.
Conscyence counseyleth both hye and lowe,
And Conscyence comenly bereth grete blame.

Blame,
Ye, and oftentymes set in shame.   305
Wherfore I rede you, men, bothe in ernest *and* in game,
Conscyence that ye knowe.

For I knowe all the mysterys of man,
They be as symple as they can,
And in euery company where I come   310
    ˙ Conscyence is out cast.
All the worlde dothe Conscyence hate.
Mankynde and Conscyence ben at debate,
For yf mankynde myght Conscyence take
    My body wolde they brast.   315

Brast, ye, and warke me moche wo.   [Aviᵛ]

MANHODE

Say, how felowe? who gaue the leue this way to go?
What, wenest thou I dare not come the to?
    Say, thou harlot, whyder in hast?

CONSCYENCE

What! let me go, syr. I knowe you nought.   320

MANHODE

No, bychyde brothell, thou shalte be taught,
For I am a knyght, and I were sought.
    The Worlde hath auaunced me.

CONSCYENCE

Why, good syr knyght, what is your name?

MANHODE

Manhode, myghty in myrthe and in game.   325
All powere of Pryde haue I tane;
   I am as gentyll as iay on tre.

CONSCYENCE

Syr, thoughe the Worlde haue you to manhode brought,
To mayntayne maner ye were neuer taught.
No, Conscyence clere ye knowe ryght nought,   330
   And this longeth to a knyght.

MANHODE

Conscyence, what the deuyll, man, is he?

CONSCYENCE

Syr, a techer of the spyrytualete.

MANHODE

Spyrytualyte, what the deuyll may that be?

CONSCYENCE

   Syr, all that be leders in to lyght.   335

MANHODE

Lyght, ye, but herke, felowe, yet lyght fayne wolde I se.

CONSCYENCE

Wyll ye so, syr knyght? than do after me.

[Bi]

MANHODE

Ye and it to Prydes pleasynge be,
   I wyll take thy techynge.

CONSCYENCE

Nay, syr, beware of Pryde and you do well,   340

For pryde Lucyfer fell in to hell.
Tyll domysdaye ther shall he dwell
    Withouten ony out comynge,

For pride, syr, is but a vayne glorye.

MANHODE

Peas, thou brothell, and lette those wordes be,   345
For the Worlde and Pryde hath auaunced me.
    To me men lewte full lowe.

CONSCYENCE

And to beware of pryde, syr, I wolde you counsayll,
And thynke on Kynge Robert of Cysell,
How he for pryde in grete pouerte fell   350
    For he wolde not Conscyence knowe.

MANHODE

Ye, Conscyence, go forthe thy waye,
For I loue Pryde and wyll go gaye.
All thy techynge is not worthe a straye,
    For Pryde clepe I my kynge.   355

CONSCYENCE

Syr, there is no kynge but God alone
That bodely bought vs with payne and passyon
Bycause of mannes soule redempcyon.
    In Scrypture thus we fynde.

MANHODE

Saye, Conscyence, syth þou woldest haue Pryde fro me,   360
What sayest thou by the kynge of Lechery?
With all mankynde he must be,
    And with hym I loue to lynge.

CONSCYENCE

Nay, Manhode, that may not be.   [Biᵛ]

From Lechery fast you fle, 365
For in combraunce it wyll brynge the
   And all that to hym wyll lynde.

MANHODE

Saye, Conscyence, of the kynge of Slouthe.
He hath behyght me mykell trouthe,
And I may not forsake hym for ruthe, 370
   For with hym I thynke to rest.

CONSCYENCE

Manhode, in scrypture thus we fynde
That Slouthe is a traytour to heuen kynge.
Syr knyght, yf you wyll kepe your kynde,
   Frome Slouthe clene you cast. 375

MANHODE

Say, Conscyence, the kynge of Glotonye,
He sayth he wyll not forsake me,
And I purpose his saruaunt to be
   With mayne and all my myght.

CONSCYENCE

Thynke, Manhode, on substaunce 380
And put out Glotonye for combraunce,
And kepe with you Good Gouernaunce,
   For this longeth to a knyght.

MANHODE

What, Conscyence, frome all my maysters þou woldes<t> haue
   m<e>.
But I wyll neuer forsake Enuy, 385
For he is kynge of company
   Bothe with more and lasse.

CONSCYENCE

Nay, Manhode, that may not be.

And ye wyll cherysshe Enuy
God wyll not well pleased be   390
    To comforte you in that case.

Bii

MANHODE

Ey, ey, from fyue kynges thou hast counseyled me,
But from the kynge of Wrathe I wyll neuer fle,
For he is in euery dede doughty,
    For hym dare no man rowte.   395

CONSCYENCE

Nay, Manhode, beware of Wrathe,
For it is but superfluyte that cometh and goeth.
Ye, and all men his company hateth,
    For ofte they stonde in doubte.

MANHODE

Fye on the, false flaterynge frere.   400
Thou shalte rewe the tyme that thou came here.
The deuyll mote set the on a fyre
    That euer I with the mete.

For thou counseylest me from all gladnes
And wolde me set vnto all sadnes.   405
But, or thou brynge me in this madnes,
    The deuyll breke thy necke.

But, syr frere, euyll mote thou thye,
Frome six kynges thou hast counseyled me,
But that daye shall thou neuer se   410
    To counsayll me frome Couetous.

CONSCYENCE

No, syr, I wyll not you from Couetous brynge,
For Couetous I clepe a kynge.
Syr, Couetous in good doynge
    Is good in all wyse.   415

But, syr knyght, wyll ye do after me
And Couetous your kynge shall be?

MANHODE

Ye, syr, my trouthe I plyght to the
 That I wyll warke at thy wyll.

CONSCYENCE

Manhode, wyll ye by this worde stande?   [Bii^v]

MANHODE

Ye, Conscyence, here my hande,   421
I wyll neuer from it fonge,
 Neyther loude ne styll.

CONSCYENCE

Manhode, ye must loue God aboue all thynge.
His name in ydelnes ye may not mynge.   425
Kepe your holy daye from worldly doynge,
 Your fader and moder worshyppe aye.

Coueyte ye to sle no man,
Ne do no lechery with no woman.
Your neyboures good take not be no waye, 430
 And all false wytnesse ye must denaye.

Neyther ye must not couete no mannes wyfe,
Nor no good that hym belythe.
This couetys shall kepe you out of stryfe.
 These ben the commaundementes ten. 435

Mankynde, and ye these commaundementes kepe
Heuen blysse I you behete,
For Crystes commaundementes ben all full swete
 And full necessary to all men.

MANHODE

What, Conscyence, is this thy Couetous?   440

CONSCYENCE

Ye, Manhode, in all wyse,
And coueyte to Crystes seruyse
   Bothe to matyns and to masse.

Ye must, Manhode, with all your myght
Mayntayne Holy Chyrches ryght,   445
For this longeth to a knyght
   Playnly in euery place.

MANHODE

What, Conscyence, sholde I leue all game and gle?

Biii

CONSCYENCE

Nay, Manhode, so mote I thye.
All myrthe in measure is good for the,   450
   But, syr, measure is in all thynge.

MANHODE

Measure, Conscyence, what thynge may measure be?

CONSCYENCE

Syr, kepe you in charyte
And from all euyll company
   For doubte of foly doynge.   455

MANHODE

Folye, what thynge callest thou folye?

CONSCYENCE

Syr, it is Pryde, Wrathe, and Enuy,
Slouthe, Couetous, and Glotonye;

Lechery the seuente is.
These seuen synnes I call folye.   460

CONSCYENCE...

MANHODE

What, thou lyest; to this
Seuen the Worlde delyuered me
And sayd they were kynges of grete beaute
  And most of mayne and myghtes.

But yet I praye the, syr, tell me,   465
Maye I not go arayde honestly?

CONSCYENCE

Yes, Manhode, hardely,
  In all maner of degre.

MANHODE

But I must haue sportynge of playe.

CONSCYENCE

Sykerly, Manhode, I say not naye,   470
But good gouernaunce kepe bothe nyght and daye
  And mayntayne mekenes and all mercy.

MANHODE

All mercy, Conscyence, what may that be?   [Biiiᵛ]

CONSCYENCE

Syr, all dyscrecyon that God gaue the.

MANHODE

Dyscressyon I knowe not, so mote I the.   475

CONSCYENCE

Syr, it is all the wyttes that God hathe you sende.

MANHODE

A, Conscyence, Conscyence, now I knowe and se
Thy cunnynge is moche more than myne.
But yet, I praye the, syr, tell me
What is moost necessary for man in euery tyme?   480

CONSCYENCE

Syr, in euery tyme beware of folye.
Folye is full of false flaterynge.
In what occupacyon that euer ye be,
Alwaye or ye begyn thynke on the endynge
  For blame.   485

Nowe fare well, Manhode; I must wende.

MANHODE

Now fare well, Conscyence, myne owne frende.

CONSCYENCE

I praye you, Manhode, have God in mynde
  And beware of Folye and Shame.   [*Exit*

MANHODE

Yes, yes, yet come wynde and rayne,   490
God let hym neuer come here agayne.
Now he is forwarde, I am ryght fayne,
  For in faythe, syr, he had nere counsayled me all amys.

A, a, now I haue bethought me, yf I shall heuen wyn,
Conscyence techynge I must begyn   495
And clene forsake the kynges of synne
  That the Worlde me taught,
And Conscyence seruaunt wyll I be
And beleue as he hath taught me   [Biiii]
Upon one God and persones thre   500
  That made all thynge of nought.

For Conscyence clere I clepe my kynge
And am his knyght in good doynge,
For, ryght of reason as I fynde,
    Conscyence techynge is trewe.   505
The Worlde is full of boost
And sayth he is of myghtes moost.
All his techynge is not worthe a coost,
    For Conscyence he dothe refuse.

But yet wyll I hym not forsake,   510
For mankynde he dothe mery make.
Thoughe the Worlde and Conscyence be at debate,
    Yet the Worlde wyll I not despyse,
For bothe in chyrche and in chepynge
And in other places beynge   515
The Worlde fyndeth me all thynge
    And dothe me grete seruyse.

Now here full prest
I thynke to rest.
Now myrthe is best.   520

                  [*Folye enters*

FOLYE

What hey, how, care awaye.
My name is Folye, I am not gaye?
Is here ony man that wyll saye naye
    That renneth in this route?

A, syr, God gyue you good eue.   525

MANHODE

Stonde vtter, felowe, where doest þou thy curtesy preue?

FOLYE

What, I do but clawe myne ars, syr, be your leue.

I praye you, syr, ryue me this cloute.

MANHODE

What, stonde out, thou sayned shrewe?   [Biiii^v]

FOLYE

By my faythe, syr, there the cocke crewe,   530
For I take recorde of this rewe
    My thedome is nere past.

MANHODE

Now trewely it may well be so.

FOLYE

By God, syr, yet haue I felowes mo,
For in euery countre where I go   535
    Some man his thryfte hath lost.

MANHODE

But herke, felowe, art thou ony craftes man?

FOLYE

Ye, syr, I can bynde a syue and tynke a pan
And therto a coryous bukler player I am.
    Aryse, felowe, wyll thou assaye?   540

MANHODE

Now truely, syr, I trow thou canst but lytell skyl of playe?

FOLYE

Yes, by Cockes bones, that I can.
I wyll neuer fle for no man
    That walketh by the waye.

MANHODE

Felowe, thoughe thou haue kunnynge   545

I counsayll the leue thy bostynge,
For here thou may thy felowe fynde
   Whyder thou wylte at longe or shorte.

FOLYE

Come, loke, and thou darest, aryse and assaye.

MANHODE

Ye, syr, but yet Conscyence byddeth me naye.   550

FOLYE

No, syr, thou darest not, in good faye,
   For truely thou faylest no false herte.   [Ci]

MANHODE

What sayst thou, haue I a false herte?

FOLYE

Ye, syr, in good faye.

MANHODE

Manhode wyll not that I saye naye.   555
Defende the, Folye, yf you maye,
   For in feythe I purpose to wete what thou art.

[Manhode and Folye fight.]

How sayste thou now, Folye, hast thou not a touche?

FOLYE

No, ywys, but a lytell on my pouche.
On all this meyne I wyll me wouche   560
   That stondeth here aboute.

MANHODE

And I take recorde on all this rewe,

Thou hast two touches, thoughe I saye but fewe.

FOLYE

Ye, this place is not without a shrewe,
 I do you all out of dewe.   565

MANHODE

But herke, felowe, by thy faythe, where was thou bore?

FOLYE

By my faythe, in Englonde haue I dwelled yore,
And all myne auncetters me before;
 But, syr, in London is my chefe dwellynge.

MANHODE

In London? where yf a man the sought?   570

FOLYE

Syr, in Holborne I was forthe brought,
And with the courtyers I am betaught.
 To Westmynster I vsed to wende.

MANHODE

Herke, felowe, why doost thou to Westmynster drawe?

FOLYE   [Ci^v]

For I am a seruaunt of the lawe.   575
Couetous is myne owne felowe;
 We twayne plete for the kynge,
And poore men that come from vplande,
We wyll take theyr mater in hande;
Be it ryght or be it wronge,   580
 Theyr thryfte with vs shall wende.

MANHODE

Now here, felowe, I praye þe whyder wendest þou than?

FOLYE

By my feyth, syr, into London I ran
To the tauernes to drynke the wyne,
 And than to the innes I toke the waye. 585
And there I was not welcome to the osteler,
But I was welcome to the fayre tapester
And to all the housholde I was ryght dere,
 For I haue dwelled with her many a daye.

MANHODE

Now, I praye þe, whyder toke þou than the waye? 590

FOLYE

In feythe, syr, ouer London brydge I ran,
And the streyght waye to the stewes I came
 And toke lodgynge for a nyght.
And there I founde my brother Lechery.
There men and women dyde folye, 595
And euery man made of me as worthy
 As thoughe I hadde ben a knyght.

MANHODE

I praye the yet tell me mo of thyne aduentures.

FOLYE

In feythe, euen streyght to all the freres,
And with them I dwelled many yeres, 600
 And they crowned Folye a kynge.

MANHODE

I praye the, felowe, whyder wendest thou tho? Cii

FOLYE

Syr, all Englande to and fro,
In to abbeys and in to nonneryes also,
 And alwaye Folye dothe felowes fynde. 605

MANHODE

Now herke, felowe, I praye the, tell me thy name.

FOLYE

Iwys, I hyght bothe Folye and Shame.

MANHODE

A ha, thou arte he that Conscyence dyd blame
    Whan he me taught.
I praye the, Folye, go hens and folowe not me.   610

FOLYE

Yes, good syr, let me your seruaunt be.

MANHODE

Naye, so mote I thye,
    For than a shrewe had I caught.

FOLYE

Why, good syr, what is your name?

MANHODE

Manhode myghty, that bereth no blame.   615

FOLYE

By þe roode and Manhode mystereth in euery game
    Somdele to cherysshe Folye,
For Folye is felowe with the Worlde
And gretely beloued with many a lorde,
And yf ye put me out of your warde   620
    The Worlde ryght wroth wyll be.

MANHODE

Ye, syr, yet had I leuer the Worlde be wrath
Than lese the cunnynge that Conscyence me gaue.

FOLYE

A cuckowe for Conscyence, he is but a dawe.   624
    He can not elles but preche.   [Cii^v]

MANHODE

Ye, I praye the, leue thy lewde claterynge,
For Conscyence is a counseler for a kynge.

FOLYE

I wolde not gyue a strawe for his techynge.
    He dooth but make men wrothe.

But wottest thou what I saye, man?   630
By that ylke trouthe that God me gaue,
Had I that bychyde Conscyence in this place
I sholde so bete hym with my staffe
    That all his stownes sholde stynke.

MANHODE

I praye the, Folye, go hens and folowe not me.   635

FOLYE

Yes, syr, so mote I thye,
Your seruaunt wyll I be;
    I axe but mete and drynke.

MANHODE

Peace, man, I may not haue the for thy name,
For thou sayst thy name is bothe Folye and Shame.   640

FOLYE

Syr, here in this cloute I knyt Shame,
    And clype me but propre Folye.

MANHODE

Ye, Folye, wyll thou be my trewe seruaunt?

FOLYE

Ye, syr Manhode, here my hande.

MANHODE

Now let vs drynke at this comnaunt,   645
    For that is curtesy.

FOLYE

Mary, mayster, ye shall haue in hast.
[*To audience.*] A ha, syrs, let the catte wyncke.
For all ye wote not what I thynke,   Ciii
I shall drawe hym suche a draught of drynke   650
    That Conscyence he shall awaye cast.

Haue, mayster, and drynke well,
And let vs make reuell! reuell!
For I swere by the chyrche of Saynt Myghell
    I wolde we were at stewes,   655
For there is nothynge but reuell route.
And we were there, I had no doubte
I sholde be knowen all aboute,
    Where Conscyence they wolde refuse.

MANHODE

Peas, Folye, my fayre frende,   660
For, by Cryste, I would not þat Conscyence sholde me here fynde.

FOLYE

Tusshe, mayster, therof speke no thynge,
    For Conscyence cometh no tyme here.

MANHODE

Peace, Folye, there is no man that knoweth me.

FOLYE

Syr, here my trouthe I plyght to the   665

And thou wylte go thyder with me.
   For knowlege haue thou no care.

MANHODE

Pease, but it is hens a grete waye.

FOLYE

Parde, syr, we may be there on a daye.
Ye, and we shall be ryght welcome, I dare well saye,   670
   In Estchepe for to dyne.
And than we wyll with Lombardes at passage playe,
And at the Popes Heed swete wyne assaye.
   We shall be lodged well and fyne.

MANHODE

What sayest thou, Folye, is this the best?   675

[Ciii^v]

FOLYE

Syr, all this is manhode, well thou knowest.

MANHODE

Now, Foly, go we hens in hast;
   But fayne wolde I chaunge my name,
For well I wote yf Conscyence mete me in this tyde
Ryght well I wote he wolde me chyde.   680

FOLYE

Syr, for fere of you his face he shall hyde.
   I shall clepe you Shame.

MANHODE

Now gramercy, Folye, my felowe in fere,
Go we hens, tary no lenger here;
Tyll we be gone me thynke it seuen yere.   685
   I haue golde and good to spende.

FOLYE

A ha, mayster, that is good chere.
And or it be passed halfe a yere
I shall the shere ryght a lewde frere,
    And hyther agayne the sende.   690

MANHODE

Folye, go before and teche me the waye.

FOLYE

Come after, Shame, I the praye,
And Conscyence clere ye cast awaye.

[*To audience.*]
    Lo, syrs, this Foly techeth aye,
For where Conscyence cometh with his cunnynge,   695
Yet Folye full fetely shall make hym blynde.
Folye before and Shame behynde —
    Lo, syrs, thus fareth the worlde alwaye.   [*Exit*

MANHODE

Now I wyll folowe Folye, for Folye is my man.
Ye, Folye is my felowe and hath gyuen me a name.   700
Conscyence called me Manhode, Folye calleth me Shame.

Folye wyll me lede to London to lerne reuell.   Ciiii
Ye, and Conscyence is but a flaterynge brothell,
    For euer he is carpynge of care.
The Worlde and Folye counseylleth me to all gladnes,   705
Ye, and Conscyence counseylleth me to all sadnes,
Ye, to moche sadnes myght brynge me in to madnes.
    And now haue good daye, syrs; to London to seke Folye
        wyll I fare.

[*Enter Conscyence*

CONSCYENCE

Saye, Manhode, frende, whyder wyll ye go?

MANHODE

Nay, syr, in faythe, my name is not so.   710
Why, frere, what the deuyll hast thou to do
    Whyder I go or abyde?

CONSCYENCE

Yes, syr, I wyll counsell you for the best.

MANHODE

I wyll none of thy counsell, so haue I rest.
I wyll go whyder me lest,   715
    For thou canst nought elles but chyde.   [*Exit*

CONSCYENCE

Lo, syrs, a grete ensample you may se:
The freylnes of Mankynde,
How oft he falleth in folye
Throughe temptacyon of the fende,   720

For, whan the fende and the flesshe be at one assent
Than Conscyence clere is clene out cast.
Men thynke not on the grete Iugement
That the sely soule shall haue at the last.

But wolde God, all men wolde haue in mynde   725
Of the grete daye of dome,
How he shall gyue a grete rekenynge
Of euyll dedes that he hathe done.

But nedeles syth it is so
That Manhode is forthe with Folye wende,   730
To seche Perseueraunce now wyll I go   [*Ciiii*^v]
With the grace of God omnypotent.

His counseylles ben in fere.
Perseueraunce counsell is moost dere.
Nexte to hym is Conscyence clere   735
    From synnynge.

Now in to this presence, to Cryst I praye
To spede me well in my iournaye.
Fare well lordynges, and haue good daye.   739
    To seke Perseueraunce wyll I wende.   [Exit

              [*Enter Perseueraunce*

PERSEUERAUNCE

Now Cryst, our comely creature, clerer than crystal clene
That craftly made euery creature by good recreacyon,
Saue all this company that is gathered here bydene,
And set all your soules in to good saluacyon.

Now good God þat is moost wysest and welde of wyttes,   745
This company counsell, comforte, and glad,
And saue all this symylytude that semely here syttes.
Now, good God, for his mercy, that all men made,

Now Mary Moder, mekest that I mene,
Shelde all this company from euyll inuersacyon   750
And saue you from our enemy, as she is bryght *and* clene,
And at þe last day of dome delyuer you fro*m* euerlastynge damp-
    nac*y*on.

Syrs, Perseruieraunce is my name,
Conscyence borne broder that is.
He sente me hyder mankynde to endoctryne   755
That they sholde to no vyces enclyne,
For ofte mankynde is gouerned amys

And throughe foly mankynde is set in shame.
Therfore in this presens to Cryst I praye
Or that I hens wende awaye   760

Some good worde that I may saye
To borowe mannes soule from blame.

[*Enter Manhode, now as Age*
[Cv]

AGE

Alas, alas, that me is wo.
My lyfe, my lykynge I haue forlorne.
My rentes, my rychesse, it is all ygo.   765
Alas the daye that I was borne.

For I was borne Manhode, moost of myght,
Styffe, stronge, both stalworthy and stoute.
The Worlde full worthely hath made me a knyght,
All bowed to my byddynge bonerly aboute.   770

Than Conscyence clere, comely and kynde,
Mekely he met me in sete there I sate.
He lerned me a lesson of his techynge,
And the seuen deedly synnes full lothely he dyde hate —

Pryde, Wrathe, and Enuy and Couetous in kynde —   775
The Worlde all these synnes delyuered me vntyll —
Slouthe, Glotony, *and* Lechery þat is full of false flaterynge.
All these Conscyence reproued both lowde and styll.

To Conscyence I helde vp my hande
To kepe Crystes commaundementes.   780
He warned me of Folye, þat traytour, *and* bade me beware.
     And thus he went his waye.
But I haue falsly me forsworne.
Alas the daye that I was borne.
For body and soule I haue forlorne,   785
     I clynge as a clodde in claye.

In London many a daye
At the passage I wolde playe.
I thought to borowe and neuer paye,

Than was I sought and set in stockes;   790
In Newgate I laye vnder lockes.
If I sayd ought, I caught many knockes.
Alas, where was Manhode tho?
    Alas, my lewdenes hath me lost.

Where is my body so proude and prest?   795
I coughe and rought, my body wyll brest,   [Cv^v]
    Age dothe folowe me so.
I stare and stacker as I stonde,
I grone grysly vpon the grounde.
Alas, Dethe, why lettest thou me lyue so longe?   800
    I wander as a wyght in wo

And care,
For I haue done yll.
Now wende I wyll
My selfe to spyll   805
I care not whyder nor where.

PERSEUERAUNCE
Well ymet, syr, well ymet, and whyder awaye?

AGE
Why, good syr, wherby do ye saye?

PERSEUERAUNCE
Tell me, syr, I you praye,
    And I with you wyll wende.   810

AGE
Why, good syr, what is your name?

PERSEUERAUNCE
Forsothe, syr, Persueraunce, the same.

AGE

Syr, ye are Conscyence brother that me dyd blame.
   I may not with you lynge.

PERSEUERAUNCE

Yes, yes, Manhode, my frende in fere.   815

AGE

Nay, syr, my name is in another maner,
For Folye his owne selfe was here
   And hath clepyd me Shame.

PERSEUERAUNCE

Shame —
Nay, Manhode, let hym go,   820
Folye and his felowes also,   [Cvi]
For they wolde the brynge in to care and wo,
   And all that wyll folowe his game.

AGE

Ye, game who so game,
Folye hath gyuen me a name,   825
   So where euer I go
He clypped me Shame.
Now Manhode is gone,
   Folye hath folowed me so.

Whan I fyrst from my moder cam   830
The Worlde made me a man,
And fast in ryches I ran
   Tyll I was dubbed a knyght.
And than I met with Conscyence clere,
And he me set in suche manere   835
Me thought his techynge was full dere
   Bothe by daye and nyght.

And than Folye met me,

And sharpely he beset me,
And from Conscyence he fet me.   840
    He wolde not fro me go.
Many a daye he keped me,
And to all folkes he cleped me
Fro Shame.
    And vnto all synnes he set me.   845

Alas, that me is wo,
For I haue falsely me forsworne.
Alas that I was borne.
Body and soule I am but lorne,
Me lyketh neyther gle nor game.   850

PERSEUERAUNCE

Nay, nay, Manhode, saye not so.
Beware of Wanhope, for he is a fo.
A newe name I shall gyue you to,   [Cvi^v]
    I clepe you Repentaunce,
For and you here repente your synne   855
Ye are possyble heuen to wynne.
But with grete contrycyon ye must begynne
    And take you to abstynence.

For thoughe a man had do alone
The deedly synnes euerychone,   860
And he with contrycyon make his mone
    To Cryst our heuen kynge,
God is also gladde of hym
As of the creature that neuer dyde syn.

AGE

Now, good syr, how sholde I contrycyon begyn?   865

PERSEUERAUNCE

Syr, in shryfte of mouthe without varyenge.

And another ensample I shall shewe you to:
Thynke on Peter and Poule and other mo,
Thomas, Iames, and Iohan also,
 And also Mary Maudeleyn. 870
For Poule dyde Crystes people grete vylany,
And Peter at the Passyon forsoke Cryst thryes,
And Maudelayne lyued longe in lechery,
 And Saynt Thomas byleued not in the Resurreccyon,

And yet these to Cryst are derlynges dere 875
And now be sayntes in heuen clere.
And therfore, thoughe ye haue trespased here,
 I hope ye be sory for your synne.

AGE

Ye, Perseueraunce, I you plyght,
I am sory for my synne bothe daye and nyght. 880
I wolde fayne lerne with all my myght
 How I sholde heuen wynne.

PERSEUERAUNCE   [Cvii]

So to wynne heuen fiue nessarye thynges there ben
That must be knowen to all mankynde.
The fiue wyttes doth begynne, 885
 Syr, bodely and sprytually.

AGE

Of the fiue wyttes I wolde haue knowynge.

PERSUERAUNCE

Forsoth, syr: herynge, seynge, and smellynge,
The remenaunte, tastynge and felynge,
 These ben the fiue wyttes bodely. 890

And syr, other fiue wyttes there ben.

AGE

Syr Perseueraunce, I knowe not them.

PERSEUERAUNCE

Now, Repentaunce, I shall you ken.
    They are the power of the soule.
Clere in mynde, there is one,   895
Imagynacyon and all reason,
Understondynge and compassyon,
    These belonge vnto Perseueraunce.

AGE

Gramercy, Perseueraunce, for your trewe techynge.
But, good syr, is there ony more behynde   900
That is necessary to all mankynde
    Frely for to knowe?

PERSEUERAUNCE

Ye, Repentaunce, more there be
That euery man must on byleue,
The twelue artycles of the fayth   905
    That mankynde must on trowe.

The fyrst, that God is in one substaunce
And also that God is in thre persones,
Begynnynge and endynge without varyaunce,
    And all this worlde made of nought.   910
The seconde, that the Sone of God sykerly   [Cvii^v]
Toke flesshe and blode of the Vyrgyn Mary
Without touchynge of mannes flesshe companye,
    This must be in euery mannes thought.

The thyrde, that that same God Sone,   915
Borne of that holy Vyrgyn,
And she after his byrthe mayden as she was beforne
    And clerer in all kynde.
Also the fourthe, that same Cryst, God and man,

He suffred payne and passyon 920
Bycause of mannes soule redempcyon
    And on a crosse dyde hynge.

The fyfte artycle, I shall you tell,
Than the Spyryte of Godhed went to hell
And bought out the soules that there dyde dwell 925
    By the power of his owne myght.
The sixth artycle, I shall you saye,
Cryst rose vpon the thyrde daye,
Very God and man withouten naye,
    That all shall deme and dyght. 930

He sent mannes soule in to heuen,
Alofte all the aungelles euery chone;
There is the Fader, the Sone,
    And þe sothfast Holy Goost.
The eyght artycle we must beleue on, 935
That same God shall come downe
And deme mannes soule at the daye of dome,
    And on mercy than must we trust.

The ninth artycle, with outen stryfe
Euery man, mayden, and wyfe 940
And all the bodyes that euer bare lyfe
    And at the daye of dome body and soule shall pere.
Truely the tenth artycle is
All they that hath kepyd Goddes seruyce,
They shall be crowned in heuen blysse [Cviii]
    As Crystes seruauntes, to hym full dere. 946

The eleuenth artycle, the sothe to sayne,
All that hath falsely to God guyded them,
They shall be put in to hell payne;
    There shall be no synne couerynge. 950
Syr, after the twelfth we must wyrche
And byleue in all the sacramentes of Holy Chyrche
That they ben necessary to both last and fyrste

To all maner of mankynde.

Syr, ye must also here *and* knowe þe commau*n*deme*n*tes ten.   955
Lo, syr, this is your beleue and all men;
Do after it and ye shall heuen wyn
      Without doubte, I knowe.

AGE

Gramercy, Perseueraunce, for your trewe techynge
Fo<r> in the spyryte of my soule wyll I fynde   960
That it is necessary to all mankynde
      Truely for to knowe.

Now, syrs, take all ensample by me,
How I was borne in symple degre.
The Worlde ryall receyued me   965
      And dubbed me a knyght.
Than Conscyence met me,
So after hym came Folye.
Folye falsely deceyued me,
      Than Shame my name hyght.   970

PERSEUERAUNCE

Ye, and now is your name Repentaunce
Throughe the grace of God Almyght.
And therfor, withoute ony dystaunce,
I take my leue of kynge and knyght,
And I praye to Ihesu whiche has made vs all,   975
Couer you with his mantell perpetuall.   Amen.

[Cviiiᵛ]
      Here endeth the Interlude of Mundus *et* Infans. Imprynted at
London in Fletestrete at the sygne of þe Son*n*e by me Wynkyn de
Worde. The yere of our Lorde M.CCCCC and xxij. The xvij daye of
July.

Textual Notes

Emendations are noted in the textual notes along with more important variant readings presented by previous editors. Expansions of abbreviations in the text are indicated by italics, and broken or missing letters are given thus: Fles<sh>e.

The following abbreviations are used in the textual notes and refer to previous editions of the play:

Chamberlin   Mallory Chamberlin, Jr. "The World and the Child, Otherwise Called *Mundus et Infans*: A Critical Edition." Unpublished dissertation. University of Tennessee, 1969.

Collier   Robert Dodsley, ed. *A Select Collection of Old Plays*, 3rd ed. Ed. John Payne Collier. 8 vols. London: Septimus Prowett, 1826. 8:307–36.

Hazlitt   Robert Dodsley, ed. *A Select Collection of Old English Plays*, 4th ed., enlarged. Ed. W. Carew Hazlitt. 15 vols. London: Reeves and Turner, 1874–76. 1:239–75.

Manly   John Matthews Manly, ed. *Specimens of the Pre-Shaksperean Drama*. 2 vols. Athenaeum Press, 1897–98. 1:352–85.

Roxburghe   Viscount Althorp (presenter). *A Proper New Interlude of the World and the Child, Otherwise Called Mundus et Infans*. Roxburghe Club. London: Shakspeare Press, 1817.

Schell   Edgar T. Schell and J. D. Schuchter, eds. *English Morality Plays and Moral Interludes*. New York: Holt, Rinehart and Winston, 1969. Pp. 167–98.

1522   *The Worlde and the Chylde, Otherwyse Called Mundus et Infans*. London: Wynkyn de Worde, 1522.

7. stalworthe] *Roxburghe;* stal worthe *1522*
9. Worlde] *Collier;* storlde *1522*
32. Forty] .xl. *1522*
33. Fles<sh>e] sh *or possibly* ch *faded out 1522;* Flesshe *Roxburghe*
36. Now] Oow *1522*
39. And] Aud *1522*

75

62. Mundus et Infans *at foot of page at sig. Aii*: *also at sigs. Aiii*, *Bi*, *Bii*, *Biii*, *Ci*, *Cii*, *Ciii*, *and Ciiii*. *All are cropped except Aiii, Bii, Biii, and Ciii.*

70. fourteen] .xiiij. *1522*

89. wrynge] r *faded 1522*

93. gynne] *Roxburghe;* gynnne *1522*

115. seu<e>n] ²e *not visible 1522*

119. þe] *1522;* that *Manly;* emperou<r>] *part of* <r> *visible 1522*

121. seuen] .vij. *1522*

127. All] Al l *1522*

138. loue] *Collier;* soue *1522*

144. nineteen] .xix. *1522*

150–51.] *Manly; lines reversed 1522*

164. Yf ony] Yfony *1522*

167. dede] *1522;* dent *Manly*

186. without lesynge] *1522;* omit *Manly*

202. Golde] d *damaged 1522*

210. a swerde] aswerde *1522*

216. peryllous] *1522; Manly suggests* pereles; yprobyde] *1522;* yprovyde *Manly;* yprouyde *Chamberlin*

222. aferde] a ferde *1522*

227. no] *Collier;* do *1522*

242. bolder] bolde *1522*

244. named] e *damaged 1522*

258. Brygaunt Ernys] *1522;* Brigand harness *Hazlitt*

260. Brestplates] st *damaged 1522*

268. vnder] v *blotted or damaged 1522; cf.* vayne *(l. 344),* vs *(l. 645)*

274. may] *tail of* y *missing 1522 (cf. ll. 389, 632)*

275–78. *1522 makes intensive use of abbreviations in these long lines to fit within margin*

277. wordely] *1522;* worthily *Lester*

278. wyll] *final* l *damaged 1522*

292. euery] *Collier;* enery *1522*

316. Brast] *possibly extra-metrical as* Blame, *l. 304, and* Shame, *l. 819*

329. maner] *1522;* maners *Manly*

348. you counsayll] *Manly;* counsayll you *1522*

374. kynde] *Manly;* kynde *or* mynde *suggested by Collier;* kynge *1522*

375. Frome] *Collier;* Rrome *1522*

377. forsake] *Collier;* for sake *1522*

384. woldes<t> . . . m<e>] t *and* e *cropped 1522;* woldest . . . me *Roxburghe*

386. company] m *faint 1522*

389. ye] *tail of* y *missing 1522*

409. six] .vi. *1522*
438. ben all] *Manly;* all *1522*
490. yet] ye *1522*
494. bethought] be thought *1522*
503. am] *Lester; omit 1522*
505. is trewe] *1522;* trewe is *Manly*
513. wyll] ¹l *faint 1522;* despyse] ²s *obscured by show-through from*
B4ᵛ 1522
515. beynge] ¹e *incomplete 1522*
519. rest] *Collier;* ro rest *1522*
522. I am] *1522;* Am I *Manly*
529. sayned] *1522;* fayned *suggested by Collier*
530. By my] *Collier;* By by *1522*
556. yf you] *Manly;* yftyou *1522;* if tyou *Roxburghe;* if thou *Lester*
565. dewe] *1522;* doute *Manly*
590. than the waye] *1522;* the waye than *Manly*
610. Folye] *Collier;* folyc *1522*
622. wrath] *1522;* wroth *Chamberlin*
632. bychyd] *tail of* ¹y *missing 1522*
633. bete] et *faint because of staining 1522*
645. comnaunt] *1522;* covenant *Schell*
657. had] *1522;* have *Manly*
660. frende] r *faint at top 1522*
674. and] a *1522;* a-fyne *Manly*
699–701. *Manly prints as six lines in trimeter, cued for song*
706. sadnes] *Collier;* sadnts *1522*
713. wyll] *Collier;* myll *1522*
715. me] *Manly;* my *1522*
746. company] y *faint 1522*
754. that] *Manly; omit 1522*
774. seuen] .vij. *1522*
777. Glotony] *Manly;* couetous *1522*
788. wolde] *part of* o *missing 1522*
799. grysly] *Manly, Chamberlin;* glysly *1522*
814. lynge] *1522;* lende *Manly*
825. a name] *Collier;* aname *1522*
843. *1522;* shame he cleped me *Lester*
844. Fro] *1522;* For *Manly; omit Hazlitt*
852. Wanhope] *Manly, following Kittredge;* wanhode *1522*
883. fiue] .v. *1522*
885. fiue] .v. *1522*
887. fiue] .v. *1522*
890. fiue] .v. *1522*

891. fiue] .v. *1522*
905. twelue] .xij. *1522;* fayth] *1522;* byleue *Manly*
913. flesshe] *1522;* flesshle *Manly, following Kittredge*
916. Borne] *1522;* [Was] born *Manly*
925. bought] *1522;* brought *Schell*
927. sixth] .vi. *1522*
931. soule] sonle *1522*
933–34.] *Manly; printed as one line 1522*
939. ninth] .ix. *1522*
943. tenth] .x. *1522*
947. eleuenth] .xi. *1522*
948. guyded] *Manly;* gayded *1522*
951. twelfth] .xij. *1522*
955. ten] .x. *1522*
960. Fo<r>] r *not visible 1522*
975. has] as *1522*

Critical Notes

ABBREVIATIONS:

Arthur: Harold Arthur, "On a MS. Collection of Ordinances of Chivalry of the Fifteenth Century, belonging to Lord Hastings," *Archaeologia* 57 (1900): 29–70.

Brand, *Observations*: John Brand. *Observations on Popular Antiquities*, new ed., rev. Henry Ellis. London: Chatto and Windus, 1913.

Chamberlin: Mallory Chamberlin, ed. *"The World and the Child, Otherwise Called Mundus et Infans*: A Critical Edition." Ph.D. diss., University of Tennessee, 1969.

Chaucer: *The Riverside Chaucer*, 3rd ed., gen. ed. Larry Benson. Boston: Houghton Mifflin, 1987.

Chester Mystery Cycle: *The Chester Mystery Cycle*, ed. R. M. Lumiansky and David Mills. EETS, s.s. 3, 9. London: Oxford University Press, 1974–86.

Coventry: *Two Coventry Corpus Christi Plays*, ed. Hardin Craig, 2nd ed. EETS, e.s. 87. London: Oxford University Press, 1957.

Davidson, *Illustrations*: Clifford Davidson. *Illustrations of the Stage and Acting in England to 1580*. Kalamazoo: Medieval Institute Publications, 1992.

Digby: *Late Medieval Religious Plays of Bodleian MSS 133 and e museo 160*, ed. Donald Baker, John L. Murphy, and Louis B. Hall, Jr. EETS, 283. Oxford: Oxford University Press, 1982.

Hanawalt: Barbara Hanawalt. *Growing up in Medieval London*. Oxford: Oxford University Press, 1993.

Hickscorner: *Two Tudor Interludes: Youth and Hickscorner*, ed. Ian Lancashire. Manchester: Manchester University Press, 1980.

Jacob's Well: *Jacob's Well*, ed. Arthur Brandeis. EETS, o.s. 115. London: Kegan Paul, Trench, Trübner, 1900.

Lancashire: Ian Lancashire, "The Auspices of *The World and the Child*," *Renaissance and Reformation* n.s. 12 (1976): 96–105.

Lay Folks' Catechism: *The Lay Folks Catechism*, ed. Thomas Frederick Simmons and Henry Edward Nolloth. EETS, o.s. 118. London: Kegan Paul, Trench, Trübner, 1901.

Lester: G. A. Lester, ed. *Three Late Medieval Morality Plays*. London: Ernest Benn, 1981.

L'Omme Pecheur: *Moralités Françaises*, ed. Werner Helmich (Geneva: Slatkine, 1980), 1:111–421.

Manly: John M. Manly, ed. *Specimens of the Pre-Shaksperean Drama*, 2 vols. Boston: Ginn, 1897–98.

Middle English Sermons from MS. Royal 18 B.xxiii: *Middle English Sermons from MS. Royal 18 B.xxiii*, ed. Woodburn O. Ross. EETS, o.s. 209. 1940; reprint

London: Oxford University Press, 1960.

Macro: *The Macro Plays*, ed. Mark Eccles. EETS, 262. London: Oxford University Press, 1969.

Mirror of the Periods of Man's Life: Hymns to the Virgin and Christ, the Parliament of Devils, and Other Religious Poems, ed. Frederick Furnivall. EETS, o.s. 24. 1868; reprint New York: Greenwood Press, 1969. Pp. 58–78.

OED: Oxford English Dictionary, 2nd ed. 20 vols. Oxford: Clarendon Press, 1989.

Oxford Dictionary of English Proverbs: The Oxford Dictionary of English Proverbs, 3rd ed., rev. F. P. Wilson. Oxford: Clarendon Press, 1970.

Sacramentum Mundi: Sacramentum Mundi, ed. Karl Rahner *et al.*, 6 vols. Herder and Herder, 1968–70.

Stow, *Survey of London*: John Stow. *The Survey of London*, ed. Charles Lethbridge Kingsford, 2 vols. Oxford: Clarendon Press, 1908.

Sugden, *A Topographical Dictionary*: Edward H. Sugden. *A Topographical Dictionary to the Works of Shakespeare and His Fellow Dramatists*. Manchester: Manchester University Press, 1925.

Towneley: *The Towneley Plays*, ed. Martin Stevens and A. C. Cawley. EETS, s.s. 13–14. Oxford: Oxford University Press, 1994.

Tilley: Morris Palmer Tilley. *A Dictionary of Proverbs in England in the Sixteenth and Seventeenth Centuries*. Ann Arbor: University of Michigan Press, 1950.

Whiting: Jere Bartlett Whiting. *Proverbs, Sentences, and Proverbial Phrases from English Writings before 1500*. Cambridge: Harvard University Press, 1968.

---

1. Manly provides a stage direction: "*Mundus, seated on his throne.*" The presence of a throne is indicated at l. 285 ("this sete") and is implied by the woodcut at the beginning of the text. The woodcut, however, was not designed specifically for this play; see Introduction.

seace of youre sawes: Conventional cry for silence at the beginning of a play.

10. All rychesse redely it renneth in me: All riches are indeed to be found in me.

11. game: This word has common associations with innocent pleasure and also with the way in which strife and contest could be circumscribed with rules.

12. in sale I sende: Mundus, seated in state, dispatches worldly pleasures.

16. I shall hym smyte with pouerte: Allegorically, the World is the distributor of wealth; to ignore his power is to invite poverty.

20. Me thynketh I am a god of grace: Mundus is thus associated with Pride, and further his statement is reminiscent of Lucifer's ambition to be like God (see l. 341). The reference to grace is ironic, since Mundus hardly qualifies as a dispenser of heavenly grace.

21. The floure of vertue foloweth me: In addition to the impertinent irony, this may suggest that there are mute followers on stage.

24. fre wyll: The more usual late medieval view of man's will holds that it is free to follow good or evil as represented by the World, the Flesh, and the Devil or the Seven Deadly Sins. Mundus, a typical tyrant, requires total obedience, however, and thus subverts Infans's will. The argument over the freedom of the will was to be a central issue at the Reformation. Luther reaffirmed the Augustinian position, which denies that the will can be free without the intervention of grace, necessary for salvation; see *What Luther Says*, ed. Ewald M. Plass, 3 vols. (St. Louis: Concordia, 1959), 3: 1443–53.

25–27. Possibly a line rhyming with "mynde" is missing here. Infans is respectfully praying for grace.

29. How mankynde doth begynne: Cf. *Mirror of the Periods of Man's Life*, l. 1: "How mankinde dooþ bigynne. . . ."

31. Goten in game and in grete synne: Cf. *Mirror of the Periods of Man's Life*, l. 3: "In game he is bigoten in synne." Sexual play, even when it results in conception, is sinful. Such an attitude toward sexuality was deeply influenced by Stoicism beginning with the early Christian period. It was a theological commonplace that sex within marriage was proper, but the expression of passionate feelings remained sinful. For the Stoic view, see R. D. Hicks, *Stoic and Epicurean* (reprint New York: Russell and Russell, 1962), 110–12.

33–34. These lines, somewhat softened, seem adapted from *Mirror of the Periods of Man's Life*, ll. 4–5: "Þe child is þe modris deedli foo;/ Or þei be fulli partide on tweyne. . . ."

35. In peryll of dethe we stode bothe two: See Introduction, above, p. 6. Childbirth was extremely hazardous both for the mother and for the child. See also *The Worlde and the Chylde*, ll. 42–43, below. For discussion, see Hanawalt, 42–45. Genesis 3:16 affirms that as a result of the Fall women shall "in sorrow . . . bring forth children."

36. Now to seke dethe I must begyn: Life is a journey which has its terminus at death; cf. *Everyman*, l. 103: "On the thou must take a longe iourney."

38. body and soule . . . shall than twynne: The separation of body and soul at death. In the visual arts, the soul is often shown as a small doll-like figure emerging from the mouth of the dying person, as in British Library Add. 37,049 (fig. 6); see also Clifford Davidson, *Visualizing The Moral Life* (New York: AMS Press, 1989), 78.

40. Fourty wekes: The period of time when the fetus was developing in the womb.

45. Poore and naked: See Job 1:21: "Naked came I out of my mother's womb. . . ." There is a suggestion here concerning Infans's costume, which presumably simulated nudity, though full nudity was, of course, unlikely. White leather was used for the nudity of Adam and Eve in the Cornish *Creacion of the World* (ed. Paula Neuss [New York: Garland, 1983]): "*Adam and Eva aparlet in whytt lether*" (l. 344 *s.d.*); see also *The Staging of Religious Drama in Europe in the Later Middle Ages*, ed. Peter Meredith and John E. Tailby (Kalamazoo: Medieval Institute Publications, 1983), 130, 146, for similar evidence from the Continent.

48. Now in to the Worlde wyll I wende: Embedded stage direction: Infans will cross the playing area and approach Mundus.

49. Some comforte of hym for to craue: Ironically the comfort offered by Mundus to the Child is also critical to his survival. See l. 62 for Infans's assertion that the World must be the source of the food and clothing essential "his lyfe to saue." Cf. *Mirror of the Periods of Man's Life*, ll. 19–20: "Þou shuldist deie for hunger and coolde/ But y lent meete *and* cloþe to þee." For the necessity of going to the World, see Introduction, n. 32; this dependency is renewed at l. 116, below.

51. God that all made: The World was created by God, who is the author of all things, at the same time that it represents the temptations that follow upon the Fall of Man. The doctrine that God made all things out of nothing was insisted upon as a standard of orthodoxy; see l. 501, below, and in expositions of the Creed—e.g., *Middle English Sermons from MS. Royal 18 B.xxiii*, 14. As Deus, who is the "maker unmade," explains prior to the Creation in the Tanners' pageant in the *York Plays* (ed. Richard Beadle [London: Edward Arnold, 1982]), "all sall be made euen of noghte" (1.9, 16). The corresponding Towneley pageant affirms even more clearly the Augustinian idea that "All maner thyng is in my thoght, / Withoutten me ther may be noght" (1.13–14).

55. Dalyaunce: A "name of no substaunce" (l. 59), as Mundus admits; it is one that was given to Infans by his mother in play. Lester observes that "in relation to a child, [the word] means 'chatter,' 'baby-talk,' 'play'; but when he grows older it will imply 'amorous talk', 'flirtation'" (113).

61–63. Infans perhaps kneels in supplication before Mundus. His request is granted on condition that he will "be obedyent to my byddynge" (ll. 65–66). Chamberlin notes (198) that kneeling before a king was customary. As a servant, Infans would expect to be taken into the household of Mundus and to receive his livery to wear.

67. garmentes gaye: A change of costume for Infans, who receives clothing representing childhood. Judging from the evidence of the visual arts, garments for children who were past infancy in the early sixteenth century seem to have been modeled on adult clothing except in the case of headgear. But "gaye" suggests frivolity.

69. Wanton: In contrast to baptism in which the child receives his name in a rite that specifically rejects vice in its renunciation formula (in the *Sarum Manuale* the renunciation of Satan, all his works, and all his pomps), here Infans obtains his name from Mundus, who represents the World. The fact that the name is to be temporary is indicative of its insubstantiality.

70. fourteen yere: In the early fourteenth century fourteen was the age at which childhood was understood to be supplanted by youth and the time when appenticeships were entered into; however, later placement of apprentices became normal in the fifteenth century. See Hanawalt, 113.

72–74. Infans leaves the presence of Mundus, but the latter remains visible in his "sale" (see l. 12).

75. rychelesnesse: Cf. Chaucer's Parson's Tale: "Thanne cometh necligence, or reccheleesnesse, that rekketh of no thyng" (*Canterbury Tales* 10.706–08).

76–118. Mundus is not directly involved in this sequence, though, as Lester suggests (115), he may well be a witness to it. See Appendix II: A Doubling Scheme.

78. toppe: Tops were popular toys from antiquity; see Brand, *Observations*, 549–50. The top was whipped into motion with a scourge (see l. 80, where the "scorge stycke" is also used to hit another child on the head). See Introduction and fig. 12.

81. My felowe vpon the heed hytte: In *Mirror of the Periods of Man's Life* the evil angel advises the child "To beete alle children" (l. 80).

83. blere on hym my tonge: Stick out the tongue as an insult. Cf. *Mirror of the Periods of Man's Life*, ll. 77–78: "Quod þe wickid aungil, 'while þou art a child,/ With þi tunge on folk þou bleere'."

87. be rewe: In a row, possibly meaning "in turn."

91. call my dame shrewe: Cf. *Mirror of the Periods of Man's Life*, ll. 71–72: "Þe wickid aungil bad him be boold/ To calle boþe fadir *and* modir shrewis."

99. This connynge came me of kynde: This skill came to me naturally, by nature (as part of his inheritance of original sin).

100. gelde a snayle: Proverbial? Cf. Thersites's fight with a snail (*Thersites*, ll. 108–10; in *Three Classical Tudor Interludes*, ed. Marie Axton [Cambridge: D. S. Brewer, 1982]).

101. catche a cowe by the tayle: Proverbial; cf. Tilley C753: "He that owns the cow goes nearest her tail."

103. I can daunce and also skyppe: Cf. *Mirror of the Periods of Man's Life*, l. 293: "I leepe, y daunce, y skippe, y synge."

104. chery pytte: In this game cherry pits were thrown into a small hole in the ground; see Brand, *Observations*, 536.

105–06. wystell you a fytte . . . in a whylowe ryne: To blow a tune on a (willow) whistle. This primitive musical instrument was a small pipe, which was held vertically like a recorder; it may have had a thumb-hole in its back as well as fingering holes in the front. Presumably the pipe was a stage prop held and played by Infans.

108–10. Thievery was commonly associated with schoolboys. Chamberlin has called attention (93) to an example used by Alexander Carpenter in his *Destructorium Viciorum* 4.2: "Now a gang of mischievous boys is robbing an apple-orchard, each vying with the other as to who shall gather the largest load, while their smaller and weaker companions look on enviously from outside, begging in vain for a share. 'But what happens?' When hoods and bosoms are full, the porter or gardener is already waiting at the gate with his stick to spoil the spoilers and send them howling home, stripped *tam pomis quam pannis*" (G. R. Owst, *The* Destructorium Viciorum *of Alexander Carpenter: A Fifteenth-Century Sequel to* Literature and the Pulpit in Medieval England [London: SPCK, 1952], 25).

112–13. Boys' reluctance to go to school was proverbial; see *As You Like It* 2.7.145–47. The schoolmaster lifts Wanton's garment to hit him directly on the flesh of his buttocks.

116. take wage: The convention for the mankind figure to go to the World is also seen for Ladolescent in *L'Omme Pecheur*, p. 116.

119. wende to the Worlde: Embedded stage direction: Wanton now will go back to Mundus and salute him. Possibly he kneels as he may have at ll. 61–63.

124–26. A newe name . . . Loue, Lust, Lykynge in fere: Glossed by Lester as "something like 'Passion and Pleasure in Love," (117), but "in fere" suggests a close link between the elements in the name. This triple-decker name signifies youth in its carefree and sensual aspects—a portion of life that will last for seven years (l. 129). Again it is Mundus who has given him his name. Cf. *Mirror of the Periods of Man's Life*, l. 35: "Lust, liking, *and* iolite." See also the Macro *Castle of Perseverance* in which a character named Lust and Liking appears.

132. as fresshe as flourys in Maye: Conventional description of the young lover; cf. Chaucer's General Prologue to *The Canterbury Tales*: "Al ful of fresshe floures . . . as fressh as is the month of May" (ll. 90–92).

134. garmentes gaye: A new set of garments, appropriate for a youth who aspires to be a young lover, is required.

138–40. I would not avoid lying in hell (or purgatory?) until the Last Judgment if only I could win my lover.

144. nineteen: "Twenty-one" would be expected, but "nineteen" fits the verse and seems to be the word that was intended.

146. go to the Worlde: Embedded stage direction; cf. ll. 48, 119.

155. One and twenty winter: At twenty-one years of age, Wanton is now about to become a man. See Introduction, p. 14.

160. Manhode myghty shall be thy name: Again Mundus gives a name to the protagonist. Hereupon Mundus encourages him to exercise his power over others. Cf. *Mirror of the Periods of Man's Life*, l. 252: "Ful of manhode *and* of myȝt"; the context there, however, is the establishment of the man's character at thirty years of age. See also *The Worlde and the Chylde*, l. 767.

161. Bere the prest in euery game: Be prepared in any eventuality; "game" suggests trickery.

170. seuen kynges sewen me: The Seven Deadly Sins are followers of Mundus. In other instances, the Seven Deadly Sins are divided in their service between the World, the Flesh, and the Devil, as in the Digby *Mary Magdalene* and the Macro *Castle of Perseverance*. On the Seven Deadly Sins, see also Morton Bloomfield, *The Seven Deadly Sins* (East Lansing: Michigan State College Press, 1952), and Introduction, pp. 6–7.

172. Pryde: First among the Seven Deadly sins; Manhode is especially drawn to him (see ll. 186–87).

179. There Pouerte is pyght: Where Poverty rules.

180–83. Lechery . . . worshyp hym aboue all thynge: Idolatry, perhaps with reference to the excesses of *Frauendienst* associated with the courtly love tradition. Lechery here is identified as male, necessary because the Seven Deadly Sins are said to be kings.

191. my trouthe I plyght: Manhode joins himself to Pride as if in marriage.

193. I swere by Saynt Thomas of Kent: An oath, invoking St. Thomas Becket, martyred at Canterbury in 1170 and, until the Reformation, the most widely venerated English saint.

194. To serue hym truely: Again offering his service, in this case to Pride, prior to receiving the garments of manhood in ll. 196–97.

197. robes ryall: Garments dyed in purple and of the appropriate material, perhaps silk. See also ll. 268–69, and Introduction, p. 12.

199. dubbe the a knyght: Manhode must kneel before Mundus in imitation of the ceremony of knighthood. He is not given his sword until l. 210. The process of creating a knight is described in a document entitled "How Knyghtis of the bath shulde be made," included as an appendix by Arthur, 67–69.

201. grace: In the worldly sense, to be distinguished from heavenly grace, which would imply the saving presence of God, either through indwelling of the Holy Spirit (Abelard) or in providing a dwelling place for the soul (Aquinas); see *Sacramentum Mundi*, 2:414.

203. Of the wrong to make the ryght: To make the worse appear better; contrast Tilley S432: "You make the better side the worse." Related to the World Upside Down *topos*, for which see Ernst Curtius, *European Literature and the Latin Middle Ages*, trans. Willard Trask (1953; reprint New York: Harper and Row, 1963), 94–98.

206. in all coloure: in all ways.

207. And now I take my leue: Manhode will leave Mundus at ll. 212–15 (he speaks these lines as he goes), then will remove himself to a different part of the stage until l. 237.

212. dubbed a knyght: With the receipt of the sword from Mundus the ceremony of dubbing is complete. He announces that he will "seke aduentures," but these will be designed "To please the Worlde in gle and game" (ll. 214–15).

223. medell erthe: Middle earth, the realm of Mundus, poised between heaven and hell in the Ptolemaic system.

224. all is at my hande werke: Blasphemous, since Mundus cannot claim to have created the world (he is not self-created).

226–27. And I . . . in the sky: If I were once angered, believe you me, no star in the sky would dare to move.

235. flourys: Possibly "floors," as suggested by Lancashire, 96; this would indicate indoor production in a hall.

245. Salerne and Samers and Ynde the Loys: Salerno, probably St. Omer (more likely than Samos in the Aegean Sea), and India the Less=Asia Minor. For this identification of Ynde the Loys, see William Caxton, *Mirrour of the World*, ed. O. H. Prior, EETS, e.s. 110 (London: Oxford University Press, 1913), 85–86. Like Salerne, Ynde the Loys was intended to invoke an exotic location. St. Omer, taken by Henry VII in February 1489, had associations with his military adventures in France. See Introduction, p. 4.

246. Caleys, Kente, *and* **Cornewayle I haue conquered clene:** Calais remained an English possession until 1558. The king landed there to pursue his French wars in October 1492. The mention of Kent and Cornwall apparently points to Henry's suppression of fifteen thousand rebels from Cornwall at Blackheath, Kent, in July 1497 as well as to his defeat of Perkin Warbeck in 1495 and again in 1497.

247. Pycardye and Pountes and gentyll Artoys: Picardy, in which St. Omer is located; Pountoise (a town north of Paris, on the Oise River); and Artois, located next to Boulogne, which King Henry besieged in 1492.

248. Florence, Flaunders, and Fraunce: Florence is probably only included for rhetorical effect, but Flanders, invaded by Lord Daubeney in 1489, is a further reference to the French wars. France was not, of course, "conquered clene" by Henry.

258. Brigaunt Ernys: Apparently a generic name for a soldier of fortune.
beten to backe *and* to bonys: Proverbial; Chamberlin, 218, cites Towneley *Processus Noe cum Filiis*, 588: "I shall bete the bak and bone."

260. as Steuen was with stonys: As St. Stephen was struck with stones at his martyrdom; see Acts 7:58–59, and the liturgy of St. Stephen, Protomartyr (26 Dec.), in the Sarum *Breviary*. The reference may be seen as an allusion to the feast of St. Stephen in the Christmas octave, when the play may have been produced (Lancashire, 97). Also, the passage ironically undercuts Manhode's bragging.

268–69. ryall arayde . . . in purpure and byse: Royal purple; garments made of fine cloth. Bis was described "as a silky linen, similar to cypress, and it seems to have been made in colours as well as white, and sometimes interwoven with gold thread" (M. Channing Linthicum, *Costume in the Drama of Shakespeare* [1936; reprint New York: Russell and Russell, 1963], 95).

272. renneth in this route: Runs with this company, perhaps indicating the audience.

276. letters: Letters patent, granting privileges.

278. They wyll me mayntayne: The reference here is to the practice of maintenance, which involved the keeping of retainers by the magnates of the realm. See the complaint of the First Shepherd in the Towneley *Secunda Pastorum*, ll. 35–36. Legislation against maintenance, especially as it served to oppress and terrorize the people, failed to eradicate the practice.

285. this sete: The seat is apparently the throne in which Mundus had been seated earlier. Manhode will refer to the seat in l. 772 when he remembers how Conscyence "Mekely . . . met me in sete there I sate." For Manhode as a kingly figure, see Introduction, pp. 12–13.

286. no loues lette I: "For no consideration will I cease" (Lester, 125)

291. That bonerly bought you on the roode tre: Christ's act of redemption on the rood tree (cross) which purchased the re-deemed from Satan. This act of exchange canceled the devil's right to all souls. See the discussion of the theology of the Atonement in Gustaf Aulén, *Christus Victor*, trans. A. G. Hebert (New York: Macmillan, 1969), 81–100.

292. praye you prestly on euery syde: Referring to the audience, invited in the following lines to pray that the devil's power be deflected.

297. heuen blysse, that hye toure: Heaven in the visual arts is often depicted as a city with walls and towers; in the Last Judgment, the city is placed at the top of the scene, with the entrance at the right hand of the Judge. In contrast is hell mouth, at the Judge's left and below. For examples, see the restored wall painting at St. Thomas of Canterbury Church, Salisbury, and the fine example dis-covered in the Guild Chapel at Stratford-upon-Avon (now in frag-mentary condition, but see the drawing by Thomas Fisher repro-duced in Clifford Davidson, *The Guild Chapel Wall Paintings at Stratford-upon-Avon* [New York: AMS Press, 1988], fig. 17).

298. nessarye: This form also appears at l. 883; the more usual "necessary" is at ll. 439, 953.

300–01. Conscyence: Conscience (from Lat. *conscientia*) is "the capacity for judging the rightness of actions, either considered generally, or actually proposed or already performed" (*The Oxford Dictionary of the Christian Church*, 2nd ed., ed. F. L. Cross and E. A. Livingston [Oxford: Oxford University Press, 1974], 335); see also *Sacramentum Mundi*, 1:414–14. Here Conscyence is dressed as a friar; see ll. 400, 408, below.

308. mysterys of man: Secrets.

315–16. brast./ Brast: For this unusual prosodic device, see Introduction, p. 23.

317. who gaue the leue this way to go? A challenge by the knight Manhode to Conscience. An embedded stage direction.

322. and: if.

327. gentyll as iay on tre: Possibly Proverbial.

329. To mayntayne maner: To be moderate.

333. a techer of the spyrytualete: Defined below as one who leads others from darkness into light (l. 335). The association of light with spiritual illumination was a medieval commonplace.

337. than do after me: Do as I do. In contrast to Mundus, who demands absolute obedience, Conscyence offers freedom from coercion and proffers the opportunity to follow his example.

341. For pryde Lucyfer fell in to hell: The conventional explanation of Lucifer's fall. See the dramatization of this event in the York and Chester plays as well as in the Towneley and N-town collections. For example, Lucifer announces in the Chester Tanners' play that he is "pearlesse and prince of pride" (*Chester Mystery Cycle* 1.184). For a useful illustration in the visual arts, see Newberry Library MS. 40, fol. 1ᵛ, containing a French translation of the *Speculum Humanae Salvationis* (Adrian Wilson and Joyce Lancaster Wilson, *A Medieval Mirror* [Berkeley and Los Angeles: University of California Press, 1984], 77, pl. III–9). The account of Lucifer's fall does not appear in Genesis but is based on Isaiah 14:12 ("How thou art fallen from heaven, O Lucifer, who didst rise in the morning"), Luke 10:18 ("and he said to them, 'I saw Satan like lightning falling from heaven'"), and Apocalypse 12:7–9.

349. Kynge Robert of Cysell: Robert of Sicily in his pride objects to the verse of the *Magnificat* that proclaims God's power to put down the mighty from their seats: *Deposuit potentes de sede*. He claims that he cannot be deposed, but shortly is replaced by an angel who takes his place on the throne. Thereafter he is treated like a court fool until finally he comes to accept his role, whereupon he is restored to his throne. See *Middle English Metrical Romances*, ed. Walter Hoyt French and Charles Brockaway Hale, 2 vols. (1930; reprint New York: Russell and Russell, 1964), 2:933–46, and Martin W. Walsh, "The King His Own Fool: *Robert of Cicyle*," in *Fools and Folly*, ed. Clifford Davidson (Kalamazoo: Medieval Institute Publications, 1996), 34–46.

354. not worthe a straye: Proverbial: "Not worth a straw" (Tilley S918).

357. That bodely bought vs with payne and passyon: Christ through his bodily suffering purchased the souls of the righteous, thereby redeeming them (l. 358); cf. commentary on ll. 924–25, below.

369. He hath behyght me mykell trouthe: He has made great promises to me.

375. Frome Slouthe clene you cast: Throw away Sloth completely.

380. substaunce: Referring to the essence of things, not to materiality.

386–87. For he is kynge ... with more and lasse: For he is a king who keeps company with both great and small. The moral point is that envy is felt by people in all ranks.

397. superfluyte: Something excessive; also, waste products from the body (*OED, s.v.* superfluity 3).

406. or: before.

413. kynge: For the allegory of kings, see Introduction, pp. 11–13.

418. my trouthe I plyght to the: Manhode now pledges himself to Conscyence.

421. here my hande: The agreement with Conscience is of a different order than his promise of service to Mundus. Here Manhode possibly raises his hand as if taking an oath and promises not to violate his promise in any way. Further corroboration of the nature of the oath-taking gesture is found in ll. 779–80 when Manhode remembers that he had "helde vp my hande/ To kepe Crystes commaundementes."

423. Neyther loude ne still: Not under any circumstances. Possibly proverbial.

424–35. The Ten Commandments fairly conventionally expounded, here as an antidote to Mundus's "commaundement" (l. 118). The teaching of the Ten Commandments, the Creed, and the Sacraments had been decreed in the Constitutions of Archbishop Peckham in 1281; see *Lay Folks' Catechism*, 14–17, 31–69, and *Middle English Sermons from MS. Royal 18 B.xxiii*, 13–15. The Ten Commandments also appear as the teachings of Jesus at age twelve in the Temple in the Coventry Weavers' pageant (ll. 971–100) and the *Chester Mystery Cycle* 11.271–98.

436–37. and ye these commandementes kepe . . . behete: If you keep these commandments, I promise you the bliss of heaven.

443. to matyns and to masse: Matins, one of the daily canonical hours, was originally sung as the night office. However, in late medieval practice Matins tended to be placed immediately before or at dawn and preceded Mass; see Karl Young, *The Drama of the Medieval Church*, 2 vols. (Oxford: Clarendon Press, 1933), 1:232. The sense here is that Conscience, a friar, urges worship of God day and night.

444–45. Ye must . . . Mayntayne Holy Chyrches ryght: The knight was required to swear to uphold both God and the Church. The order for the Knights of Bath specified that "ye schall love god above all thinge and be stedfaste in the feythe and sustene the chirche and ye scall be trewe un to yowre soveregne lorde and trewe of yowre worde and promys *and* sekirtee in that oughte to be kepte" (Arthur, 68).

449. so mote I thye: As I might thrive.

451. measure is in all thynge: Proverbial; see *Oxford Dictionary of English Proverbs*, 529; Tilley M806; Whiting M464.

Chamberlin notes that "[t]he principle of measure in all things is the main topic of the first section of Skelton's *Magnyfycence.*"

456–60. Folye: Folye involves the combination of all seven of the Deadly Sins in one figure in both *Mirror of Man's Life* and the play; see Introduction, p. 6.

468. In all maner of degre: Referring to Manhode's question "Maye I not go arayde honestly?" (l. 466). Sumptuary laws required clothing consistent with one's position in the social order; see L. F. Salzman, *English Industries in the Later Middle Ages,* 2nd ed. (Oxford: Clarendon Press, 1923), 243, citing legislation of 1363. Conscyence has no objection to Manhode's wearing garments appropriate to his station in life.

474. dyscrecyon: In *Everyman,* Discretion appears as a character.

476. wyttes: Five wits bodily and spiritual, which together establish "all dyscrecyon that God gaue the" (l. 474). The five wits bodily, listed at ll. 888–89, are the five senses, while the wits spiritual or inwits, which belong to Perseueraunce and which represent the "power of the soule," are Mind, Imagination, Reason, Understanding, and Compassion (ll. 894–98). See also the *Lay Folks' Catechism,* 18–19, and the Macro morality *Wisdom,* which makes extensive use of the five wits. According to the sermon collection *Jacob's Well,* 216–19, the bodily senses are gateways to the soul wherein the corruption of sin may enter, while the spiritual senses (in this work identified as Understanding, Desire, Delight, Mind, and Will) likewise need to be protected from the sources of wickedness (ibid., 222–23). See also Lester, 153.

484. or ye begyn thynke on the endynge: Proverbial; see Tilley, E128; Whiting, E84; cf. *Everyman:* "in the begynnynge,/ Loke well, and take good heed to the endynge" (ll. 10–11).

490–91. come wynde and rayne,/ God let hym neuer come here agayne: A conventional formula; cf. Whiting, W300: "Come wynde, come reyne, come he never a-gayne." As soon as Conscyence leaves the stage, Manhode wishes that he should never return. But he will shortly recognize that if he is to achieve salvation, he will need to attend to Conscyence's teachings and be his servant (1. 498). This deliberately incoherent speech (ll. 490–520) will provide evidence of Manhode's instability and susceptibility to temptation by the forces associated with the World.

499–500. beleue . . . Upon one God and persones thre: The Creed required belief both in the unity of God and in the three persons of Father, Son, and Holy Spirit. The mystery was illustrated in the Arms of the Trinity, as shown here:

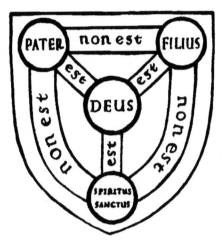

See also M. D. Anderson, *History and Imagery in British Churches* (London: John Murray, 1971), 93–94. Any denial of the Trinitarian position was regarded as heresy; see 1. 908.

501. That made all thynge of nought: God created all things *ex nihilo*. See also the exposition of the Creed, esp. 1. 910, and commentary on 1. 51, above.

504. ryght of reason: Invoking right reason as a guiding principle in life. Right reason points out the truth of Conscyence's teaching.

510–17. Manhode decides not to despise the World since pleasure and prosperity have been derived from it. The World has done him "grete seruyse" in the church, the marketplace, and elsewhere.

514. chepynge: Any marketplace, but perhaps specifically

Cheapside in London. Cheapside, or The Cheap, was located north-east of St. Paul's Cathedral (see Map).

519. I thynke to rest: Chamberlin suggests that Manhode rests by seating himself in the throne.

521. What hey, how, care awaye: Folye probably sings a fragment of a song at his entrance.

526. Stonde vtter: stand back; cf. "stonde out" (l. 529).
where doest þou thy curtesy preue? Folye does not approach Manhode with the expected courtesy and thus merits a reprimand. The gesture described in the next line provides a further example of Folye's ill behavior.

527. I do but clawe myne ars: A gesture of insult, sometimes compounded, as in the illustration of the martyrdom of St. Apollonia in Jean Fouquet's Hours of Etienne Chevalier, by exposing the buttocks to the one being insulted (see fig. 17).

528. ryue me this cloute: Literally "tear apart this rag (or piece of clothing) for me." In view of the previous line, the meaning and stage action here are probably obscene.

529. stonde out: Cf. l. 526, above.

530. By my faythe: The first of many oaths sworn by Folye, in line with the convention elaborated in later interludes by a variety of evil characters, especially the Vice. Some of them became comic formulae for avoiding charges of blasphemy, as in "by Cockes bones" (l. 542).
there the cocke crewe: The time has come; proverbial.

531. For I take recorde of this rewe: I call this company (referring to the audience) to be witnesses.

537. craftes man: Class of men skilled in crafts such as the carpenters, shoemakers, etc., who may be eligible to join a craft guild.

538. bynde a syue and tynke a pan: According to Lancashire, this may be a covert reference to William Empson, whose father was reputed to have been a sievemaker; see Introduction, p. 4, above. Chamberlin, 230, cites the comment by John Bromyard that tinkers' garments seem to be more in need of mending than their pots (*Summa Predicantium*, s.v. "Correctio"). The trade associated here with Folye thus suggests a ragged appearance, which is consistent with his role as a fool. It will be learned (l. 641, below) that he wears an outer garment which is symbolic of Shame. For the disrepute in which tinkers were generally held, see *OED*, *s.v.* tinker.

539. bukler player: The reference is to buckler play, a game in which two men fight with blunt-edged swords and bucklers as a spectator sport. The object was to draw blood and at the same time to avoid serious injury. Boys substituted cudgels for swords and wicker baskets for bucklers. See Brand, *Observations*, 533.

540. Aryse, felowe, wyll thou assaye? A challenge to Manhode to fight.

541. lytell skyl of playe: Folye promises to be a clumsy player, as we would expect of a Fool.

548. at longe or shorte: Folye may choose either a long sword (rapier) or a short sword. The use of the rapier had been newly introduced into England in the early sixteenth century, and Manhode, as Lester explains, "claims superiority in the use of both new-style and traditional weapons" (137). But Folye presumably has no sword here, and is making a comic play with his stick or bauble (see l. 633).

552. thou faylest no false herte: You cannot be said to be brave.

558. hast thou not a touche? A touche is a hit, sustained by Folye, whose ineptitude in fencing is quickly proven.

559. pouche: Perhaps the customary fool's bag or pouch. For examples, see Davidson, *Illustrations*, figs. 89 (Will Summers, in the *Psalter of Henry VIII*) and 91 (Richard Tarlton); Leslie Hotson, *Shakespeare's Motley* (London: Hart-Davis, 1952), 102 (Robert Armin).

560–61. On all this meyne . . . That stondeth here aboute: Folye appeals to the play audience in denying that he has sustained a hit. He will very quickly sustain another.

563. thoughe I saye but fewe: Though I say but little about it.

565. I do you all oute of dewe: Manhode absolves Folye of his duty; a winner of the fight will not be named.

567. yore: Usually defined as "a long time ago," the word could also signify "for a long time."

571. Holborne: Lawyers' district, lying to the west of the London city walls outside Newgate (see Map) and also known for its taverns and low life. See Sugden, *A Topographical Dictionary*, 252–53.

573. Westmynster: The seat of government, likewise also known for low life. Numerous taverns, inns, and alehouses—at least twenty along King Street—and extensive prostitution marked life in Westminster in the early sixteenth century; see Gervase Rosser, *Medieval Westminster, 1200–1540* (Oxford: Clarendon Press, 1989), 122–33, 143–44. Not insignificantly one lane leading off King Street was called Thieving Lane, and the precincts of Westminster Abbey nearby served as a commodious sanctuary for felons and debtors who sought protection from the law.

575–81. Folye and Couetous, like Empson and Edmund Dudley in the time of Henry VII, engage in legal maneuvering that will benefit their own interests at the expense of others. The merit of a case—that is, whether right or wrong—does not concern them so long as they can make a profit from it.

581. Theyr thryfte with vs shall wende: Their wealth shall come our way.

583. London: The City, as opposed to the suburbs outside the walls.

585. innes: May refer to the Inns of Court, or legal training institutions comparable to universities, but more likely to the ordinary inns or hostelries of the city where Folye would be welcome to the tapster—but not to the osteler, possibly because, as he was not a gentleman, he had no horse.

591. ouer London brydge I ran: Folye crossed London Bridge, the single walkway over the Thames. Construction on this stone bridge, which by 1500 was built up on each side so that it seemed more like a street than a bridge (see fig. 3), was begun in 1176. It was over nine hundred feet in length and had a drawbridge to allow vessels to pass. Congestion on the bridge was severe, and this might have complicated the prospect of running across it.

592. stewes: Brothels, on the Bankside in Southwark; see Introduction, above, p. 5, and fig. 4. These could be approached by boat; landings were conveniently available at the Goat Stairs, at one end of the Bankside, as well as Horseshoe Alley Stairs and, at the other end, the Bank End Stairs. The brothels may have been called "Stews" because of their apparent origin as public hot air bath houses; cf. Old French *estuve* = stove (*OED*). Prior to the temporary closing of the brothels by Henry VII in 1506 there had been eighteen houses, thereafter reduced to twelve (*The Great Chronicle of London*, ed. A. H. Thomas and I. D. Thornley [London: George W. Jones, 1938], 331). For allowed brothels, see Hampshire Record Office MS. ECI/85, 1, as cited by Martha Carlin, *Medieval Southwark* (London: Hambledon Press, 1996), 224. According to Stow, *Survey of London*, 2:55, the front of each house, facing the Thames, had a painted sign—e.g., Boar's Head, Cardinal's Hat, Cross Keys, Castle, Swan, Crane, Bell, Gun. The Bull and the Hartshorn are named in *Hickscorner*, l. 901. The Cardinal's Hat was among the brothels that remained closed; see Skelton, "Why Come Ye Nat to Courte?" ll. 237–39 (in John Skelton, *The Complete English Poems*, ed. John Scattergood [New Haven: Yale University Press, 1983]).

597. As thoughe I hadde ben a knyght: Another reminder that Folye is of lesser status; but the line also points to folly in knights.

599–601. Folye then went to a friary where he lived for "many yeres." They chose him as a mock king. (For the practice of choosing and crowning mock kings, see Sandra Billington, *Mock Kings in Medieval Society and Renaissance Drama* [Oxford: Clarendon Press, 1991]). The satire of mendicant and monastic orders is a medieval commonplace in poetry and the visual arts, and is not necessarily proto-Protestant.

611. let me your seruaunt be: A reversal of the situation earlier in the play when Mundus demanded full obedience in *his* servant.

624. A cuckowe for: Proverbial phrase?

628. not gyue a strawe: Cf. comment on l. 354, above.

633. so bete hym with my staffe: Probably with his fool stick.

634. That all his stownes stynke: Proverbial; cf. Heywood's *Johan Johan* (in John Heywood, *Plays*, ed. Richard Axton and Peter Happé [Woodbridge: D. S. Brewer, 1991]): "Bete her, quoth a? Yea, that she shall stynke" (l. 12).

638. I axe but mete and drynke: Instead of wages, only food and drink; a common arrangement.

641. in this cloute I knyt Shame: He has been wearing a garment, probably a cloak, which represents Shame. In the next line, however, he announces that he henceforth will merely be "propre Folye." Lester suggests thus that "the garment of Shame, cast off by Folly at this point, becomes available for Manhood when he assumes the name Shame . . ." (142).

645. let vs drynke at this comnaunt: Having shaken hands on the agreement to allow Folye to serve Manhode, they now will drink as a way of sealing the covenant. The drink is offered by Folye as "draught" that will lead Manhode away from Conscyence (ll. 650–51). A drinking vessel is required as a stage prop.

648–49. let the catte wyncke . . . thynke: Proverbial: "When the cat winks little wots the mouse what the cat thinks" (Tilley C176); see also *Oxford Dictionary of English Proverbs*, 109; Whiting C96.

654. chyrche of Saynt Myghell: Several churches in London were dedicated to St. Michael, including St. Michael Cornhill, St. Michael Crooked Lane, and St. Michael Paternoster; see H. B. Walters, *London Churches at the Reformation* (London: S.P.C.K., 1939). If Lancashire's hypothesis is to be entertained, it is useful to know that Earl Grey's London lodgings were either in or near the parish of St. Michael Cornhill (see Map).

656. reuell route: riotous reveling, lacking in decorum.

663. Conscyence cometh no tyme here: Folye ironically promises Manhode that where they are going Conscience will not be present.

667. For knowlege haue thou no care: As to knowledge, don't give it a thought.

669. we may be there on a daye: London is a day's journey away. Lancashire suggests a location at Ampthill, Bedfordshire, which was about this distance in time from the metropolis; see Introduction, p. 6.

671. Estchepe: Eastcheap, dominated by Butchers, was also the location of a number of cooks' establishments. The area is described in the fifteenth-century poem "London Lackpenny," formerly attributed to John Lydgate (*A Selection of the Minor Poems*, ed. J. O. Halliwell [London: Percy Society], 106):

> Then I hyed me into Est-Chepe;
> One cryes rybbs of befe, and many a pye;
> Pewter pottes they clattered on a heape;
> There was harpe, pype, and mynstrelsye.

The west end of this street was later the location of the Boar's Head Tavern which Shakespeare uses in *1* and *2 Henry IV* as the site of Falstaff's depravity: *Hal.* "Doth the old boar feed in the old frank?" *Bardolph.* "At the old place, my lord, in Eastcheap." See Sugden, *A Topographical Dictionary*, 165.

672. Lombardes: Lombards, concentrated on Lombard Street (see Map), were bankers and commercial agents. See also Stow, *Survey of London*, 1:201–02, 2:307. Earl Grey's London residence was in Lombard Street at the sign of the George; see Lancashire, 102.

at passage playe: A dice game in which two players use three dice; Joseph Strutt explains: "The caster threw continually till he had thrown doublets under ten, when he was out and lost; or doublets over ten, when he *passed* and won" (*The Sports and Pastimes of the People of England*, new ed., rev. J. Charles Cox [1903; reprint Detroit: Singing Tree Press, 1968], 247–48]). For a suggestion concerning the possible topical significance of gambling, see Lancaster, 100–01. In the play Manhode is financially ruined and will return in despair as Age.

673. Popes Heed: The Pope's Head tavern was located on Pope's Head Alley, running between Lombard Street and Cornhill. The tavern and adjacent houses are described by Stow as "strongly builded of stone" and apparently at once time "pertaining to some great estate, or rather to the king of this Realme" (*Survey of London*, 1:199). See Map.

676. manhode: This editorial choice to print "manhode" in lower case inevitably obscures the play on manhode/Manhode which would originally have been apparent when the word was heard but not seen on the page.

689. I shall the shere ryght a lewde frere: I shall shear you like an ignorant friar. (Friars were, of course, tonsured.) That is, Manhode is set up to be fleeced.

698. thus fareth the worlde alwaye: Proverbial?

699. The change of rhythm here is indicative of Manhode's submission to Folye.

709. Manhode, frende: Conscyence recognizes Manhode in spite of his disguise as Shame.

715. I wyll go whyder me lest: Manhode will go wherever he pleases. His newfound freedom is, of course, an illusion.

721. the fende and the flesshe: The Devil and the Flesh, conventionally joined with the World to form the infernal triad of the World, the Flesh, and the Devil; see Siegfried Wenzel, "The Three Enemies of Man," *Mediaeval Studies* 29 (1967): 47–66.

723. the grete Iugement: The Last Judgment, which men like to put out of mind. The scene as popularly imagined, following the account in Matthew 25, was often painted over the chancel arch of parish churches; see commentary on l. 297, above. For discussion of the morality play and Doomsday, see David Bevington, "'Man, thinke on thine endinge day'," in *Homo, Memento Finis: The Iconography of Just Judgment in Medieval Art and Drama* (Kalamazoo: Medieval Institute Publications, 1985), 147–77.

727. grete rekenynge: At the Last Day of history there will be an accounting that will balance one's evil deeds against one's good. In *Everyman* preparation for this accounting is central to the drama, for Everyman is commanded to prepare for a final "rekenynge" (l. 99) and, at the end of a terminal pilgrimage, "grete accountes before God to make" (l. 551).

733. His counseylles ben in fere: His advice gives close support.

739. Fare well lordynges: Spoken to members of the audience.

740. To seke Perseueraunce: Conscyence could not be on stage with Perseueraunce if a single actor played both roles. See Introduction, pp. 24–25, and Appendix II, below. The link between Conscyence and Perseueraunce, however, is important and will be noted in the text at ll. 753–55 when the latter announces that he is Conscyence's "borne broder," who has sent him to "endoctryne" Manhode. Perseueraunce is suggested by Matthew 10:22, which is quoted in the Macro *Castle of Perseueraunce* following l. 1705: "Qui perseuerauerit usque in finem, hic salvus erit." As Lester notes, Perseueraunce therefore should be seen as "the *remedia*, or 'antidote', of Wanhope" (146).

741–52. Alliterative verse, rhymed.

741. clerer than crystal clene: Crystall is a clear unbreakable rock (*OED*) and hence functions to define Christ in his purity and stability.

747. symylytude that semely here syttes: Reference to an audience that is sitting, not standing around, at the performance. The passage is further corroboration for performance in a hall. See also Lancashire, 96.

750. euyll inuersacyon: The implication is that evil is the reverse of the good. Instead of evil as a principle of distortion, as in Platonic philosophy, it is a force that literally turns things upside down—a condition that is related to the World Upside Down *topos*.

760. Or that: Before.

763–66. Manhode, identified in the speech tag as Age, does not at first see Perseueraunce. His lament is similar to *Mirror of the Periods of Man's Life*, ll. 337–44, 361–404.

776. The Worlde all these synnes delyuered me vntyll: The World delivered me over to all these (Deadly) Sins.

778. both lowde and styll: Completely.

779. I helde vp my hande: A vow; see note to l. 421, above. Manhode has, of course, "falsly . . . forsworne" (l. 783).

786. I clynge as a clodde in claye: I waste away like a dead body in the ground.

788. At the passage: At dice; see comment on l. 672, above.

791. Newgate: Newgate, the London city gate used as a prison until the eighteenth century (fig. 5), held sixty-four inmates in 1414 (Stow, *Survey of London*, 1:36–37). While notorious for holding dangerous criminals, its clientele also included debtors. Food and bedding were not provided for the prisoners, and the death rate was high. The prison was extremely noisy and filthy, and all the inmates were in irons except for debtors with debts under 100*s* who were able purchase their freedom (Margery Bassett, "Newgate Prison in the Middle Ages," *Speculum* 18 [1943], 240–48). In *Hickscorner*,

Imaginacion says of Hickscorner: "And in Newgate we dwelled together,/ For he and I were both shackled in a fetter" (ll. 236–37).

795. Where is my body so proude and prest? Lester, 149, suggests that the "words and the sentiment derive from the *ubi sunt* laments, moral poems consisting of long catalogues of rhetorical questions beginning *ubi sunt* . . . ('where are . . . ?') relating to the transcience of wealth, health, beauty, and other worldly things." For a classic statement, see *English Lyrics of the XIIIth Century*, ed. Carleton Brown (Oxford: Clarendon Press, 1932), 85–87, and for background see J. E. Cross, "*The Sayings of St Bernard* and *Ubi sount qui ante nos fuerount*," *Review of English Studies*, n.s. 9 (1958): 1–7.

800. Dethe, why lettest thou me lyue so longe? A sign of Manhode's despair. Death would have been imagined as he was depicted in the Dance of Death—that is, as an ugly cadaverous figure—on the cloisters of St. Paul's Cathedral and elsewhere. A woodblock showing Death in his conventional form was selected for making up the illustration on the title page of *Everyman* in the editions published by John Skot; see Davidson, *Illustrations*, 132–33. In *Everyman*, Death threatens with his dart (l. 76), and in the Macro *Castle of Perseverance*, l. 2842, he uses a dart to bring the life of the protagonist to an end. Death holds a spear and bell in an illustration in British Library MS. Harl. 1706, fol. 19^v; see Clifford Davidson, "Stage Properties and Iconography in the Early English Drama," *Mediaevalia* 15 (1993 [for 1989]): 243–46, fig. 1, and also Joan Steffeck and Clifford Davidson, "A Late Pictorial Analogue to a Scene in *The Castle of Perseverance*," *EDAM Newsletter* 12 (1990): 31–33.

805. My selfe to spyll: He contemplates suicide, which was conventionally linked with despair. Thus the figure representing Despair on a frieze at Notre Dame Cathedral in Paris is directly opposed to Hope and is stabbing herself. At Auxerre Cathedral Despair kills herself before the figure of Patience. See Adolf Katzenellenbogen, *Allegories of the Virtues and Vices in Mediaeval Art*, trans. Alan J. P. Crick (London: Warburg Institute, 1939), 116, fig. 72; and Emile Mâle, *Religious Art in France: The Thirteenth Century*, trans. Marthiel Mathews (Princeton: Princeton University Press, 1984),116, fig. 70. The convention linking despair and self-murder is also suggested in the Macro play of *Mankind*, ll. 800–05. Judas was regarded as a prime example whose suicide was caused less by his betrayal than by the fact that he fell into the deadly sin of despair; see *Jacob's Well*, 114.

818. Shame./ Shame: For versification, see Introduction, pp. 21–24, and Appendix I.

824. game who so game: Let those who want to play about.

825–28. The allegory is emphatic here, and is extensively reviewed in the following lines, up to l. 850. While Folye has given him the name of Shame, it is clear that this is a false name and that its function has been to turn Manhode's life upside down. It is significant that Shame does not appear in the speech prefixes, and that instead the protagonist is identified as Age. Nevertheless, his belief that his name is Shame leads him to wanhope and thoughts of suicide.

845. vnto all synnes he set me: He (Folye) induced me to commit all the deadly sins.

852. Wanhope: Despair, regarded as a subdivision of Accidia. See *Jacob's Well*, 114: "wanhope wyll makyn a man to holdyn hymself so synfull *and* cursed, þat hym thynketh þat he may noȝt ben amendyd, *and* þat he is so feble, þat he may wythstonde no temptacyoun, but sufferyth þe feend, þe world, *and* þe flesch, to haue here wylle, *and* . . . demyth him-self to be dampnyd." He thus refuses Confession and repentance, and "heldyth it a gret foly to prayin, or to fastyn, to ȝevyn almes, or to don ony good dede."

855. For and: And if.

857. grete contrycyon: Repentance, required for Confession if one is to be given absolution and if one is to have hope of salvation; see ll. 859–64. It must be based in love of God rather than in fear of purgatory or hell to be efficacious. It is a response to the offering of God's grace, therefore, rather than an act of selfish self-preservation or of mere remorse. See *Jacob's Well*, 176–77, and *Sacramentum Mundi*, 2:1–2.

858. abstynence: As penance.

863–64. gladde of hym / As of the creature that neuer dyde syn: Apparently a reference to the parable of the Prodigal Son. For persons who are contrite of heart and receive absolution, the stains of their sin are washed away as if they had never existed. The same doctrinal point is made by Conscience in *Mirror of the Periods of Man's Life*, ll. 548–52:

> If a manne have synned longe bifore,
> And axe mercy And a-mend his mys,
> Repente, and wilne to synne no more,
> Of þat man God gladder is
> Þan of a child synlees y-bore.

According to the *Lay Folks' Catechism*, absolution "Clenses us and wasshes us of alkyn synnes" (66).

866. shrift of mouthe: Confessing one's sins to a priest, required at least once each year by the Fourth Lateran Council (1215). Like sincere and inward contrition, shrift is integral to the Sacrament of Confession. Also necessary is penance (satisfaction). See Thomas Aquinas, *Summa Theologica*, Suppl. QQ. 12–15; *Jacob's Well*, 183–88, 195; Robert of Brunne, *Handlyng Synne*, ed. Frederick Funivall, EETS, o.s.119, 123 (1901–03; reprint Millwood, N.Y.: Kraus, 1988), 335–39.

868–74. Mary Magdalene and the apostles, with the exception of Judas, were sanctified though they had sinned, some of them greatly. Peter denied Christ three times at the time of the Passion (l. 872; Matthew 26:69–75, Mark 14:66–72, Luke 22:55–62), and Paul persecuted Christians prior to his conversion (l. 871; Romans 9:1–27). Thomas denied the Resurrection (l. 874) until he saw and touched the living Christ (John 20:24–29). Along with Peter and John, James the Great was a witness to the Transfiguration and the first of the apostles to become a martyr; an alleged relic (his hand) was displayed at Reading, and his cult was enhanced through the popularity of pilgrimage to his shrine at Compostela. John almost always appeared as one of the figures, along with the Virgin Mary, on the rood placed above the entrance to the chancel of churches prior to the Reformation. Still, it is not clear why the names of James and John were chosen by the playwright, unless he had in mind their desertion, along with the rest of the apostles, when Jesus was arrested prior to his crucifixion. Mary Magdalene—actually a composite figure made up of the sister of Martha and Lazarus, the woman from whom Christ cast out seven devils, and the penitent who came to Jesus at the house of Simon—had an extensive legendary history, including her early life "in lechery"; see Jacobus de Voragine, *The Golden Legend*, trans. William Granger Ryan, 2 vols. (Princeton: Princeton University Press, 1993), 1:375–76, and, for a dramatization, the Digby *Mary Magdalene*. The development of her legend and iconography is surveyed by Marjorie M. Malvern, *Venus in Sackcloth: The Magdalen's Origins and Metamorphoses* (Carbondale: Southern Illinois University Press, 1975).

885–86. fiue wyttes . . . bodely and sprytually: See commentary on l. 476, above.

893. Repentaunce: In a final act of renaming, Perseueraunce here first uses the name of Repentaunce in addressing Age. See below, ll. 971–72.

896. Imagynacyon: Through imagination one might visualize things absent: "þerin þingis þat þe vttir witte apprehendiþ withoute beþ i-ordeyned and iput togedres withinne" (Bartholomaeus Anglicus, *On the Properties of Things*, trans. John Trevisa, 2 vols. [Oxford: Clarendon Press, 1975], 1:98). Here one of the five inward wits. See also Chaucer, *Boece* 5.4.157:59: "the ymaginacioun comprehendith oonly the figure withoute the matere." In *Hickscorner* Imagination is a disreputable character who has been involved in transgressive acts and has spent time with the protagonist in Newgate, where both were in chains (ll. 236–37).

905. twelue artycles of the fayth: The Nicene Creed, divided into twelve clauses. Each clause could be associated with one of the apostles in the visual arts; see Nicole Mezey, "Creed and Prophets Series in the Visual Arts," *EDAM Newsletter* 2, no. 2 (1979): 7–10. Dramatic presentations of some type were staged at York and Beverley; see Alexandra F. Johnston, "The Plays of the Religious Guilds of York: The Creed Play and the Pater Noster Play," *Speculum* 50 (1975): 55–90, and Stephen K. Wright, "The York Creed Play in the Light of the Innsbruck Playbook of 1391," *Medieval and Renaissance Drama in England* 5 (1991): 27–53. For other Continental Creed plays, see Lynette R. Muir, *The Biblical Drama of Medieval Europe* (Cambridge: Cambridge University Press, 1995), 259, n. 2.

907. one substaunce: God, though a Trinity, is indivisible; see also commentary on ll. 499–500, above. The term 'substaunce' does not refer to a material creature but to the divine essence.

909. without varyaunce: God is eternal and unchanging.

910. all this worlde made of nought: The world was created out of nothing; a rejection of the view that the world was shaped out of primordial chaos or out of pre-existing atoms. See commentary on l. 51, above.

911–13. The Incarnation involved the taking of a true human body from Mary his Mother, but he was conceived without the stain of original sin that would have been communicated through sexual intercourse ("flesshe companye"). A *Stanzaic Life of Christ*, ed. Frances A. Foster, EETS, o.s. 166 (London: Oxford University Press, 1926), explains that an angel reported to Joseph "that child [Jesus] was not by mon,/ but geten thurȝe þe Holy Gost" (ll. 305–06); the *Lay Folks' Catechism* says that Christ was conceived "withowte mannys genderynge" (16). Mary's purity was further enhanced by the belief in her Immaculate Conception which was widespread in England; see Frederick G. Holweck, "Immaculate Conception,"

The Catholic Encyclopedia, 7:674–81.

917. she after his byrthe mayden as she was beforne: Mary was a virgin both before and after Christ's birth. The point is frequently emphasized, as in the antiphon *Alma redemptoris mater*; for the text and transcription of the Sarum music of this antiphon, see Beverly Boyd, *The Prioress's Tale*, A Variorum Edition of the Works of Geoffrey Chaucer, 2, pt. 20 (Norman: University of Oklahoma Press, 1987), 15–16.

924–25. the Spyryte of Godhed went to hell / And bought out the soules: The Harrowing, in which the "Spyryte of Godhed" descended into hell to rescue the souls of the righteous who had previously lived. The *Lay Folks' Catechism* in its exposition of the Creed affirms that Christ's "sowle went to helle and tok out þe sowlys/ þat he ordeynyd to saue" (17). The event is dated four thousand years after the death of Adam in the lyric poem "Adam lay I-bowndyn" (*Religious Lyrics of the XVth Century*, ed. Carleton Brown [Oxford: Clarendon Press, 1939], 120). The iconography of the Harrowing invokes a reversal of the Fall; thus in a restored wall painting at Pickering, North Yorkshire, Jesus typically is reaching out to grasp Adam by the forearm, while Adam in turn holds out in his hand the apple, which he is returning to Christ (G. H. Lightfoot, "Mural Paintings in St. Peter's Church, Pickering," *Yorkshire Archaeological Journal* 13 [1895]: 367). The word "bought" in the play's exposition may be a printer's error, but it is not inappropriate nevertheless since the death of Christ on the cross was held to involve a purchase of the souls in Limbo from the powers of darkness; see ll. 357–58, above. For discussion of the Harrowing in drama, see Clifford Davidson, *From Creation to Doom* (New York: AMS Press, 1984), 135–51, and for a general survey of the origin of the tradition see J. A. MacCulloch, *The Harrowing of Hell* (Edinburgh: T. and T. Clark, 1930).

932. Though Lester, 155, proposes adding a line which should read "He (Christ) ascended into heaven," the verse is metrically complete, and the theological point that Christ made possible man's ascent into heaven is established.

942. at the daye of dome body and soule shall pere: At Doomsday the body and soul will again be joined together. The Creed affirms the resurrection of the body, and in the visual arts bodies, often still in their winding sheets, are shown rising from their graves in preparation for the Last Judgment.

950. no synne couerynge: In hell sins are fully exposed; no hypocrisy is possible. The pains of hell are graphically illustrated in the woodcuts in *The Kalender of Shepherdes* (ed. H. Oscar Sommer, 3 vols. [London: Kegan Paul, Trench, Trübner, 1892]) which assign a different (but equally terrifying) punishment to each of the Seven Deadly Sins.

952. all the sacramentes: The Seven Sacraments—Baptism, Confirmation, Eucharist, Penance, Marriage, Ordination, Extreme Unction—were affirmed by the late medieval Church and, in spite of challenges from Lollards, were generally accepted. See Ann Eljenholm Nichols, *Seeable Signs: The Iconography of the Seven Sacraments* (Woodbridge: Boydell and Brewer, 1994), 90–128 and passim.

955. commaundementes ten: The Ten Commandments are summarized above (ll. 424–35).

971–72. now is your name Repentaunce/ Throughe the grace of God Almyght: The name Shame is now erased through God's grace, which will either bring Age-Repentaunce back to wholeness or, in keeping with the final line of the play, cover his imperfections so that at the Last Day he will achieve salvation in spite of what he has failed to accomplish in his lifetime.

976. Couer you with his mantell perpetuall: Perseueraunce addresses the audience with these words, which, as Chamberlin notes (245), are echoed in *John the Evangelist* (London: John Waley, n.d. [c.1520]): "That lorde whiche is princypall/ Conserue and kepe this congregacyon,/ And couer you with his mantell perpetuall" (sig. B1ᵛ). These words are a reminder of baptism, at which a new garment was given to the child with the words "N., receive a white robe, holy and unstained, which thou must bring before the tribunal of our Lord Jesus Christ, that thou mayest have eternal life and live for ever and ever" (*Manuale ad usum percelebris ecclesiae Sarisburiensis*, ed. A. Jefferies Collins, 2 vols. [London, 1960], 2:37; as quoted in translation in E. C. Whitaker, *Documents of the Baptismal Liturgy* [London: SPCK, 1970], 247).

Appendix I:
Verse Structures

The verse forms are here divided into three groupings, with the third including all forms that do not somehow fit into the other two. Variants of the stanza form abab and of tail-rhyme stanzas rhyming aaabcccb are described within those categories; * denotes incomplete tail-rhyme stanzas.

abab		aaabcccb	Other
1–16	Mundus		
17–20	Mundus		
(abaa)			
21–24	Mundus		
25–27	Infans		
(aba)			
28–51	Infans		
		52–75 Mundus, Infans	
		76–99 Wanton [sol]	
		100–06 Wanton	
		(aabcccb)	
		107–22 Wanton	
		123–30 Mundus	
131–38	Lust L		
			139–43 Lust L
			(abbca)
		144–59 Lust L, Mundus	
		160–67 Mundus	
		(aaababac)	
		168–83 Mundus	
184–87	Manhode		
		188–211 Mundus, Manhode	
212–15	Manhode		
216–31	Mundus		

abab	aaabcccb	Other
		232–36 Mundus (abbba)
237–48 Manhode		
		249–53 Manhode (abbba)
254–61 Manhode		
		262–66 Manhode (abbba)
	267–82 Manhode (Kings)	
		283–87 Manhode (abbba)
288–303 Conscyence		
		304–07 Conscyence (aaab)
	308–15 Conscyence	
	316–19 Manhode, Conscyence (aaab*)	
	320–399 Conscyence, Manhode	
	400–07 Manhode (aaabcccd)	
	408–23 Manhode, Conscyence	
	424–31 Conscyence (aaabccbb)	
	432–455 Conscyence, Manhode	
	456–64 Manhode, Conscyence (aaababaac)	
	465–72 Manhode, Conscyence (aaaa bbba)	
	473–76 Manhode, Conscyence (aaab*)	
477–80 Manhode, Conscyence		
481–85 Conscyence (ababc)		
	486–93 Conscyence, Manhode (aaab cccd)	
	494–517 Manhood	
		518–20 Manhode (aaa)
	521–36 Folye, Manhode	
	537–44 Manhode, Folye (aaabbaab)	

abab	aaabcccb	Other
	545–48 Manhode (aaab*)	
	549–57 Folye, Manhode (aaabbaaab)	
	558–65 Manhode, Folye (aaaabcccc)	
	566–89 Manhode, Folye	
	590–97 Manhode, Folye (abbcdddc)	
	598–629 Manhode, Folye	
	630–38 Folye, Manhode (abcbdeeed)	
	639–45 Manhode, Folye	
		647–51 Folye (abbba)
	652–67 Folye, Manhode	
	668–74 Manhode, Folye (aaabccb)	
	675–90 Manhode, Folye (aaabbbc)	
	691–98 Manhode, Folye (aaaabbba)	
		699–701 Manhode (aaa)
	702–08 Manhode (aabcccb)	
	709–16 Manhode, Conscyence	
717–32 Conscyence		
	733–40 Conscyence [sol] (aaabcccd)	
741–52 Perseveraunce		
	753–62 Perseveraunce (abccb addda)	
763–78 Age [sol]		
	779–86 Age [sol] (aabcdddc)	
	787–93 Age (aaab bbc)	
	794–801 Age	
		802–06 Age (abbba)

abab	aaabcccb	Other
	807–14 Perseveraunce, Age	
	815–23 Perseveraunce, Age	
	(aaab[b]cccb)	
	824–29 Age	
	(aabaab)	
	830–37 Age, Perseveraunce	
	838–45 Age	
	(aaabaa[c]a)	
		846–50 Age
		(abbbc)
	851–90 Perseveraunce, Age	
	891–98 Perseveraunce, Age	
	(aaabcccd)	
	899–906 Age, Perseveraunce	
	(aaabccdb)	
	907–46 Perseveraunce, Age	
	947–54 Perseveraunce	
	(aaabcccd)	
	955–70 Perseveraunce, Age	
971–74 Perseveraunce		
		975–76 Perseveraunce
		(aa)

Appendix II:
A Doubling Scheme

Line	Player A	Player B
1	Mundus	
25	Mundus	Infans
	Mundus	(72) Wanton
76	[Mundus]	Wanton
123	Mundus	(131) Lust L
	Mundus	(184) Manhode
216–36	Mundus	
237		Manhode
288	Conscyence	Manhode
490		Manhode
521	Folye	Manhode
699		Manhode
709	Conscyence	Manhode
717–40	Conscyence	
741		Perseveraunce
763–976	Age	Perseveraunce

Note: At ll. 236 and 740 the stage is cleared. The ensuing pauses could be very short, or they could be extended into substantial intervals. If the second were a long one, Conscyence and Perseveraunce could be played by Player A, and Player B could stick to the human roles throughout.

Appendix III:
The Dialect
of *The Worlde and the Chylde*

By Paul A. Johnston, Jr.

The extant copy of the early sixteenth-century play *The Worlde and the Chylde* comes at a transition period in English linguistic history. It was printed by Wynkyn de Worde at a time when the Chancery Standard had, in broad outline, been adopted.[1] However, there was still much variation in orthographic conventions and even to some extent in morphology so that texts can be placed, though this may not be done as easily as in, say, the early fifteenth or fourteenth century. The problem of placing a text such as *The Worlde and the Chylde* is somewhat similar to determining where a Central Midland Standard document comes from, which likewise can be done using cluster analyses and comparison to spellings in the *Linguistic Atlas of Late Middle English* (*LALME*).[2] While the purview of the *Linguistic Atlas* supposedly ends in 1450, there are a few later manuscripts included, and many of the spellings shown might be expected to die away slowly, replaced by what would become the Standard form.

In some cases, there is an even better source of evidence. De Worde, like Caxton before him and most of his contemporaries, was an editor as well as a printer, and one of his jobs entailed putting manuscripts into a dialect already conventionally accepted as suitable for a mass market: London Chancery English. The results of his editing reduce the prevalence of non-Chancery spellings greatly and confine the investigator to looking at the occasional departure from Chancery practice rather than the most common orthography. However, a verse work such as *The Worlde and the Chylde* will show its original rhymes more or less intact, even if the spellings may not be, since altering them entails changing the work entirely. I can only see one case where something like this might have happened: the word *dede* when the form *dent* "dint" might have made sense and a proper rhyme to boot (l. 167).

However, rhyme evidence merely shows proximity, not necessarily identity, and this is particularly true of this work, though there seem to be rules to these "near rhymes," namely:

1. Voiceless stops may appear in the same set of rhymes with other voiceless stops: cf. ll. 80–82, *stycke/hytte/skyppe*; ll. 312–14, *hate/debate/take.*
   2. Clusters of nasal + voiced stop may rhyme with other such clusters: ll. 359, 363, 367, *fynde/lynge/lynde*; ll. 420–22, *stande/hande/fonge* (see below).
   3. Nasals may participate in rhymes with each other: ll. 537–39, *man/pan/am.*
   4. Short and long vowels of similar quality may rhyme: ll. 387, 391, *lasse/case.*

Bearing this in mind, we can probably say the following about the phonology of the dialect:

1. Both the top and bottom halves of the Great Vowel Shift have begun to apply, though just barely, since ME /e: i:/ and /o: u:/ may freely rhyme: ll. 172–74, *pryde/dede/abyde;* ll. 936–37, *downe/dome.* The likely values would be something like /i: u:/ for the old high-mid vowels and /ëi öu/ for the old high ones (and cf. *denaye = deny,* l. 431).
   2. ME /a:/ has gone, variably, to /ɛ:/ l. 675–77, *best/knowest/hast.*
   3. /a/ before nasal + /d/, but not before nasal alone, goes to /ɔ/: *stande/hande/fonge,* as above; ll. 228, 230, *londe/wronge.*
   4. The distinction between final /ɔ: o:/, but not the two vowels in other positions, is neutralized: ll. 851–53, *so/fo/to*; ll. 316–19, *wo/go/to.* The first apparently has not raised, as it rhymes with short /o/ before voiceless fricatives: l. 506–08, *boost/moost/coost* (*cost*).
   5. ME /ɛ:r/ = /e:r/, but isolative /ɛ: e:/ are distinct in other positions: ll. 123–25, *dere/here/fere.*
   6. ME /eu/ = /ɛu/: ll. 562–65, *rewe/fewe/shrewe/dewe.*
   7. ME /ɔxt/ = /axt/: ll. 320–22, *nought/taught/sought.*
   8. /x/ is weak or deleted: ll. 179–79, 183, *lolyte/pyght/myght.*
   9. /r/ is gone in syllable codas before alveolars and dentals: ll. 144–46, *olde/bolde/worlde;* ll. 176–77; *fourte (fou'the); slouthe (=sleuth,* "deception," rather than *sloth).*
   10. OE /y(:)/ has occasionally become /ɛ e:/ alongside /ɪ i:/ ll. 486–88, *wende/frende/mynde* (mende). This happens more commonly for long /y:/ than short /y/.

11. *Take* has a long vowel, *came* and *gone* (=/a/!) a short one (*cam:man:ran*, ll. 830–32).

12. ME /u/ may be lowered to something like /ɔ/ on its way to /ʌ/: ll. 110, 113, *plucke/docke*;

13. The following forms are implied by rhymes: *felawe* for *felowe*; *worle/worde* for *worlde*; *thaym* for *them*; *clipe* for *clepe*; *feer* for *fyre*; *ga* (=[ɑː]) for *gaue*; *cherche* for *chirche*; *frynd* for *frend*. In addition, forms like *sholde* for *should, lasse* for *less*, and *than* for *then* are expressly found.

14. A few prefixed participles like *ypyght, ygo* appear.

The combination of all these factors indicate a quite specific area. The fact that ME /ɔː/ is always rhymed and written as a back round vowel, as in *moost* above, excludes the North. Forms like *knowe* instead of *knawe* likewise excludes both the North and Kentish. Since *good* is generally *good/gode*, not *goud*, and there is no trace of initial voiceless fricatives being written with <v, z>, the Southwest is eliminated. West Midland documents would have <o> from /a/ before single nasals as well as /nd/ clusters, and would have *then* not *than*. Characteristics 7, 11, 12, and forms like *lasse* indicate the Southern half of the East Midlands, while 3, 4 , and 8 point to an area within East Anglia, as does the implied form *gan* for *gone*. The /yː/ > /eː/ forms suggest that Central or Eastern Norfolk is to be excluded, as you get /iː/ there. The region cannot be too far South, however, as the implied form *felawe* only appears as far south as Central Cambridgeshire.

In fact, there are a few items which assure a provenance in Cambridgeshire, or possibly West Suffolk or extreme Southwest Norfolk. *Word* for *world,* implied in line 618; *wyrche* for the verb "work," *fet* for "fetch," and *yinge* for "young" combined with the above-mentioned *felawe,* and *lasse,* according to the dot maps in *LALME*, vol. 1, clinch this location for the original manuscript used by the printer. It could have conceivably come from Cambridge city itself, or smaller centers nearby like Ramsey, Chatteris, or Newmarket, but probably not the Isle of Ely or the interior of Norfolk. Since some of these forms have discontinuous distributions in *LALME*, the center or even east of Suffolk (Bury St. Edmunds, Ipswich) is a possibility, though the fit is not as good as the more westerly area.

We can see here that, even with the regularization that de Worde probably imposed on the manuscript of *the Worlde and the Chylde*, it is nevertheless still possible to make at least a tentative geographical assignment by comparing the spellings and implied rhymes with the *LALME* records, since Standardization, though present, was still somewhat incipient during the early years of Henry VIII's reign. This suggests that linguists used to working with Middle English manuscripts could profitably turn their attentions to early Tudor times, and that they might use similar methodologies to localize works from this very fertile transition period.

NOTES

[1] See John H. Fisher *The Emergence of Standard English* (Lexington: University Press of Kentucky, 1977), 121–40.

[2] Angus McIntosh, Michael L. Samuels, and Michael Benskin, *Linguistic Atlas of Later Medieval English*, 4 vols. (Aberdeen: Aberdeen University Press, 1986).

Glossary

The glossary is designed to assist readers by defining words that are archaic or unfamiliar. Line references are provided except for those words which appear frequently and about which there will be no confusion. Abbreviations refer to the *Oxford English Dictionary* (*OED*) and *Middle English Dictionary* (*MED*).

adred afraid for (her) life 42.

aferde terrified 222.

alofte above 932.

also as 863.

and if 226, 322, 338, 378, 389, 436, 549, 562, 657, 666, 861.

apperelde adorned 134.

assaye *v.* make trial of 109; attempt 147; assail (in fencing) 549; try, test 673.

auaunced promoted 323, 346.

auncetters ancestors 568.

axe ask 638.

aye always 428, 694.

bare behaved 241; bore 941.

behete *v.* promise 437.

beholde consider 28.

behyght promised 154, 369.

behynde still to come 900.

belythe belongs 433.

ben are; *p.pl.* been.

bere the conduct yourself 161, 211.

beset trapped, tried to destroy 839.

betaught put in the care of 572 (*MED* **bitechen** *v.* 2a).

bete *v.* beat 166, 633; beten

p.pl. beaten 258, 260.

bethought me realized 494.

ble appearance 242.

blere on mock 83.

blynne desist from, stop 143.

bodely in the flesh 357, 886, 890.

bonerly humbly 2, 229, 291, 770.

boost boasting 506.

bore *p.pl.* born 566.

borowe secure with pledge 762 (*MED* **borwe** *v* 1).

bost proud behavior 143.

bostynge bragging 546.

bounte strength 169.

boure small inner room 121; **bourys** *pl.* 234.

brast shatter 315, 316.

brest burst 796.

broder brother 754.

brothell scoundrel 321, 345, 703.

bukler player fencer 539 (*MED* **bokeler** 1).

bychyde accursed 321, 632.

byddeth *v.* commands 550.

byddynge *n.* command 2, 66, 157, 229, 770.

bydene together 743.

byse high quality linen 269.

can *v.* know, be skillful at 77;
    canst 541.
care trouble 704, 802, 822.
care, out of truly 220 (*MED*
    care 4a).
carpynge complaining 704.
case circumstance(s) 19, 25,
    391.
chepynge *n.* market 514.
chery pytte children's game
    with cherry stones 104.
claterynge chattering 626.
clawe scratch 527.
claye mud 786.
clene *adv.* completely 246, 375,
    496, 722; *adj.* pure 741,
    751.
clepe *v.* name 69, 355; **cleped**
    called 843.
clere free from, unguilty 301,
    330, 693, 722, 735, 771,
    834, 895; perfect 296, 876.
clerer more pure 741, 918.
clodde lump of earth 786.
clothe clothing 62.
cloute lump (of dirt) 528, 641.
clynge wither, shrivel 786
    (*MED* **clingen** 2a).
clype *v.* call, give name to 642;
    clypped called 827.
Cockes bones by God's bones
    (sanitized oath) 542.
coloure circumstances 206.
combraunce misfortune 366;
    sinfulness 381.
comely noble 50; handsome,
    attractive 220, 289; holy
    741, 771 (*MED* **comli** 2b).
comnaunt agreement 645.

connynge trick 99, 102; *see
    also* **kunnynge**; *cf.*
    cunnynge.
coost *n.* throw 508 (*MED* **cast**
    1a; as for dice).
coryous expert 539.
couent company 295.
couetous Covetousness or
    Avarice.
coueyte *v.* desire 428, 432, 442.
Couetys *n.* covetousness 434.
counsayll, counsell advise 348,
    411, 546, 713, 746;
    counsayled 493; **coun-
    seyleth, counseylleth** 302,
    705, 706.
craftes man member of craft
    guild 537 (*MED* **craft** 7).
craftly *adv.* skillfully 742.
craue beg 49, 61.
creature creator 741.
crystall *n.* clear, unbreakable
    rock 741.
cunnynge knowledge 478, 623,
    695; *cf.* **connynge,
    kunnynge.**

dale valley 224.
dalyaunce small talk, gossip
    55, 56.
dawe jackdaw, i.e., stupid
    fellow 624.
debate, at in conflict 313, 512.
deedly deadly 774, 860.
delyuered . . . vntyll handed
    over to 776.
deme *v.* judge 930, 937.
denaye renounce 431.
dere *v.* hurt 274.
derlynge dear one 123;
    derlynges beloved (of
    God) 875.

dewe debt, responsibility 565.
dint blow 274.
do caused (to be) 264; done 859.
docke tail of clothes (*OED* **dock** *sb.* 3b) 114
dome judgment 726, 752, 937, 942.
doubte *n.* fear 455; uncertainty 399, 657, 958.
doughty bold 173, 394.
doughtly skillfully 274.
doughtynesse strength 167.
dout *v.* fear 273.
downe hill 224.
dyght prepared 274; save 930 (*MED* **dighten** *v.* 1c.a).
dyscresyon knowledge of right and wrong 474, 475.
dyspylde spilled 254.
dystaunce discord 973.

eche every 218.
elles *adv.* in addition to 625, 716.
encreace enlarge 158.
endoctryne instruct 755.
entent will, intent, pleasure 122, 165, 194, 277.
euerychone every (single) one 860, 932.
eyen eyes 219.

fare prosper 235; **fareth** fares, prospers 698
fare *adj.* distant 243.
faye faith 551, 554.
fayre attractive.
fayne *adj.* eager 492; *adv.* eagerly 189, 336.
felde battlefield 261.
fell fierce 261.

felowe companion; **felowes** (similar) companions 605.
felyng feeling 889.
fende fiend 720, 721.
fere, in together 125, 683, 733, 815.
fest event 113 (*MED* **feste** 4a); **sory fest** sad thing 113.
fet fetched 840.
fetely *adv.* craftily 696 (*MED* **fetli**).
flourys flowers 132.
flourys floors of rooms (*MED* **flor** n1) 235.
fode food 33.
fode young woman 137 (*MED* **fode** 3b); **fodys** peoples, races 4 (*MED* 2a).
folowe follow 24, 610, 635, 699, 797; attend to 823; **foloweth** accompanies 21.
fonge flee 422.
for in the presence of 577.
forlorne *p.pl.* lost 764, 785.
forsworne *p.pl.* broken an oath 783, 847.
forwarde gone away 492.
founde provided for 32 (*MED* **funden** 15b); *v.* proceed 34 (*MED* **founden** v1.1); *v.* discovered 92, 94, 594.
fourte fourth 176.
fre noble 137.
frely readily 40; completely 902.
frere friar 400, 408, 689, 711; **freres** *pl.* 599.
freylnes feebleness 718.
fro from 360, 841; after 844.
fynde provide for 65; *see* founde 32.

fytte tune 105.

game *n.* revelry 11, 69, 140,
215, 306, 325, 448, 850;
pleasure 31, 127; contest
161.
game *v.* play 824.
gaye *adj.* splendid 67, 134, 522;
adv. splendidly 353.
gelde castrate 100.
gentyll noble 208, 247, 327.
gere armor 270.
glad *v.* make glad 746.
gle sport 127, 140, 215, 448,
850.
glyster glitter 270.
good provisions, property 430,
433, 686.
goten begotten 31 (*MED* **geten**
v. 1.17).
gouernaunce authority 149;
self control 382, 471.
grace power 20, 732 (*MED* 5c);
favor 27, 201, 972.
gramercy thank you.
grome inferior man 259.
grone groan 799.
grysly hideous 273; hideously
799.
guyded them behaved themselves 948.
gynne contrivance (?toy) 93.

hardely boldly 467.
harlot scoundrel 319.
haunte ... to *v.* practice 200.
heed head 81, 255, 673.
hende with knightly qualities
212.
hens hence.
here hear 955.

hewe color 197.
heygher more elevated 147.
hole whole, entire 165.
hyght (is) called 177, 188, 607,
970.
hynge hang 922.

imagynacyon power to form
mental images 896.
inuersacyon turning inward
750.
iolyte happiness 178.
ioyen rejoice 187.
ipreuyd well proved 217 (*MED*
preven).
ipyght established 217 (*MED*
picchen 2c).
iwys certainly 145, 607.

ken reveal 893.
kene alert 250.
kepe maintain, retain 149, 374,
382, 426, 453, 471; obey
436, 780.
keped kept prisoner 842.
knowlege recognition 667.
knyt bundle up 641 (*MED*
knitten 2c).
kunnynge 545; *see also*
cunnynge.
kyke kick 86.
kynde *n.* nature 99, 374; *adj.*
natural 75; **in kynde** for
the flesh 775; **in all kynde**
in every respect 918.

lasse *n.* those of lower rank 387
(*MED* **lesse** 3a).

leder ruler, leader 228; **leders**
pl. 335.

lene make feeble 252 (*MED*
    lener v2).
lenger longer 684.
lerned instructed 773 (*MED*
    4a).
lese lose 623.
lest *n.* pleasure 715; **lest, me** *v.*
    pleases me 112.
lesynge telling lies 184, 186;
    make a lesynge invent lies
    97.
let, lette *v.* forbear 138, 286
    (*MED* **leten** 12); **lette be**
    disregard 345 (*MED* **leten**
    18b).
letters letters patent, giving
    authority 276.
lewde ignorant 626, 689;
lewdnes, lewdenes ignoble
    behavior 128, 794.
lewte submit 347 (*MED* **lowten**
    2a).
leuer rather 622.
leuery support, sustenance 281.
lokes locks (hair) 135.
Lombardes financiers from
    Lombardy, North Italy 672.
londe land 163, 218, 228;
    londes *pl.* 240.
longe long sword 548.
longeth belongs 331, 383, 446.
lorne *p.pl.* ruined 849 (*MED*
    lesen 8).
lothely *adv.* fiercely 774.
louely *adv.* graciously 276;
    attractive 135.
lyketh, me pleases me 850.
lyfte raise 114.
lynde go 367 (*MED* **lenden** 2).
lynge *v.* stay 363, 814 (*MED*
    lengen 2).

makyde matched 262 (*MED*
    maken v. 2, and cf.
    macchen).
maner proper conduct 329
    (*MED* 5b).
mayne strength of mind 195,
    379; authority 243, 278,
    464 (*MED* **main** 1b).
mayntayne exhibit 329.
medell erthe the earthly world
    223.
mene 749 remember (*MED*
    menen *v.* 1.4a)
mete *n.* food 62, 638.
mete *v.* meet 403, 679.
meue speak 26.
meyne assembly 560.
mo more 95, 534, 598, 868.
mone prayer for forgiveness
    861 (*MED* **mon** 1b).
more *n.* persons of high station
    387 (*MED* **more** 6; cf.
    lasse *supra*).
mote might, be allowed 402,
    408, 449, 475, 612, 636
    (*MED* **moten** v2).
mowe mock, or make faces 96
    (*MED* **mouen** v2).
mought might 187; *cf.* **mote**
    supra).
myghtes strength 464, 507.
myghtly *adv.* fully 159, 231
    (*MED* **mightli** 1f).
mykell, mykyll *adj.* great 175,
    253, 369 (*MED* **muchel**).
mynge recollect 425 (*MED*
    mingen 3).
mystereth has need of 616.
mysterys hidden ways 308.

naye denial 929.

ne nor 242, 423.

nedeles nevertheless 729.

nere *adv.* nearly 493, 532.

nessarye necessary 298, 883 (rare variant *OED*).

on syde aside 294.

ony any.

or before 406, 484, 688, 760.

osteler innkeeper 586.

paleys palace 6.

parde indeed (*lit.* by God) 669.

parte bestow 17 (*MED* **parten** 8); separate 43.

passage a dice game 672, 788.

passyon suffering 357, 920; (Christ's) Passion 872.

peas, pease peace 237, 238, 345, 660, 668.

pere appear 942 (*MED* **peren** 1).

peryll danger 35.

peryllous causing fear 216, 217 (*MED* **perilous** 1).

perys pears 110.

pethely strongly 217 (*MED* **pithili**).

playe *n.* pleasure, enjoyment 469, 541.

playnly specifically 447.

pleasynge pleasure 338.

plesynge good will 151.

plete plead (legal term) 577.

plommes plums 110.

plyght *v.* pledge, swear 191, 418, 665, 879.

possessyon control and protection 41.

pouche pouch 559.

powerly piteously 47 (*MED*

povreli 3c).

praye beg 151, 198.

prest ready 161, 275, 518, 795.

prestly earnestly 292 (*MED* **prestli** 2a).

preue prove genuine 526.

propre real 642.

prycked tormented 47 (*MED* **priken** 2b).

purpure royal purple silk 269.

pyght placed, embedded 179.

pyteously *adv.* in a manner causing pity 254.

quaynte ingenious 77.

recreacyon making again, remaking 742.

rede advise 306 (*MED* **reden** 8).

redely certainly 10, 272 (*MED* 2).

renneth goes about wildly 10, 93, 272, 524 (cf. *MED* **rennen** 2).

rente financial income 163; **rentes** *pl.* 765.

reuell revelry, usually disorderly 142, 653, 656, 702.

reuen rob 268.

rewe *n.* company 531, 562; **all be rewe** one after the other 87 (*MED* **reue** 4a).

rewe *v.* regret 401.

roode 616; **roode tre** 291 Christ's cross.

rought make a noise, ?belch 796 (*MED* **routen** v.3).

route company 272, 524, 656.

rowte make trouble, cry out 395 (*MED* **routen** v.3).

ruthe pity 370.
ryall royal 197, 268, 965.
ryallest most royal 272.
rychelesnesse rashness 75.
rychesse wealth 10, 765.
rychest most opulent 232.
ryne, whylowe pipe made from willow twig 106.
ryotte debauchery 142.
ryse branches, hedges 268 (*MED* **ris** 1c).
ryue *v.* tear 528.

sale great hall 12.
same, in in the same way 78, 133.
sawes talking 1, 238.
sayne tell 947.
sayned holy (an oath) 529.
scole school 108, 112.
scorge stycke whip stock 80.
scyence knowledge 147.
se throne 22.
se, you care for you 51 (*MED* **sen** 23a).
see sea 225.
seche seek 731.
sely foolish 724 (*MED* **seli** 2).
semely splendid 12, 22, 28, 747; handsome 133, 209.
sende dispatch 12, 281, 690; *p.pl.* 476.
sete seat, place 772; place of government 285 (*MED* 2c).
sette sit 22; fixed 136.
sewen attend upon 170.
shapen shaped 133.
sharpely forcefully 166, 294, 839.
shere shave the head 689.
shorte short sword 548.

shrewe scold 91 (*MED* **shreu** 3); devil 529, 564, 613 (*MED* **shreu** 2).
shryfte of mouthe auricular confession 866.
skyl knowledge 541 (*MED* **skil** 7).
sle kill 428.
so provided that 66, 714.
somdele greatly 617 (*MED* *adv.* 3).
sore passionately 136.
sothe truth 947.
sothfast true, just 934.
sought checked 322; looked for 570, 790.
spyll kill 805.
spyrytualete doctrine, devotional practice 333 (*MED* **spiritualte** 2).
sprytually piously, with devotion 886.
stacker stagger 798.
stalworthe, stalworthy strong 7, 239, 271, 768.
stare stare wildly 222, 798.
stere stir 227.
sterre star 227.
stewes brothels 592, 655.
stonde stand 399, 526, 529, 798; **stondeth** stands 227, 561.
stownes testicles 634.
stowpe bend over 231.
stowte bold 239.
straye straw 354.
strayte narrow 37.
stretes streets 8.
strondes seashores 8.
styffe resolute 271, 768.
styll *adv.* quiet 423, 778.

substaunce worth, substance 59, 150; permanent spiritual wealth 380 (*MED* 5a); divine essence 907 (*MED* 2b).

superfluyte immoderate behavior 397.

sykerly certainly 470, 911.

symylytude company 747.

syth since 360, 729.

syue strainer, sieve 538.

tale, in in specific words 226.

tane taken 326.

tapester barmaid 587.

tell until 138.

tene annoy 251.

than then (*except* 478, 623, 741).

tho then 33, 602, 793.

the thrive 475; *see also* **thye.**

thedome prosperity 532 (*OED* cites this line).

there where 255, 772.

thryfte prosperity, (good) fortune 536, 581 (*MED* **thrift** a, b).

thye prosper 408, 449, 612, 636.

touche blow received 558 (*MED* 1b); **touches** *pl.* 563.

toure tower 297; **toures** *pl.* 233.

trouthe promise 191, 631; commitment 369, 418, 665 (*MED* **treuth** 2a).

trow believe 541; **on trowe** believe in 906.

twayne two 577.

twynne *v.* separate 38.

tyde time 190, 679.

tynke mend, solder 538 (*OED* v²).

varyaunce change 909.

varyenge argument, doubt 866.

vntyll unto 776.

vplande rural areas 578.

vtter further away 526.

wage, take be employed 116.

warde protection 620.

walketh extends 265.

warke work 316, 419.

wanhope sinful despair of forgiveness 852.

waxe grow 145, 213; **waxest** grow 58.

wayte well take care 162 (*OED* 1e).

wayte the lie in wait for you 164 (*OED* **wait** *v.* 1b).

wayteth me waits for me 230.

welde powerful 745 (*OED* **wield** *adj.* 1).

wende, wendest go.

wenest think 318.

went clothed 46.

wete know 557.

wherby why 808.

whyder whither.

whylowe *see* **ryne** 106.

wolde, woldest would.

wonder wonderfully 145, 213, 265.

wordely worthily 277.

worthely worthily 46, 769.

wote know 9, 53, 649, 679, 680; **wottest thou** do you know? 630.

wouche assert, certify 560 (*OED* 5).

wrapped clothed 46.
wroth, wrothe angry 621, 629.
wrought done 185 (ME **wir-
chen** *p.pl.*: cf. **wyrche**).
wrynge with contort, wrest out
of position 89.
wyght man 282, 283, 284, 801.
wyght strong 267.
wyghtly nimbly 82.
wylde inappropriate 57.
wyrche work 951.
wystell *v.* whistle 105.

wyttes intelligence and the
senses 476, 745, 885, 887,
890, 891.

ydyght prepared, defended 8.
ygo gone 765.
ylke same 631.
ymet met 807.
yinge young 65.
yore a long time ago 567.
yprobyde well proved 216.
ypyght established 6, 217.